Inner Art of Vegetarianism

Meditations on the Inner Art of Vegetarianism

Spiritual Practices for Body and Soul

Carol J. Adams

Lantern Books • New York
A Division of Booklight Inc.

Lantern Books
One Union Square West, Suite 201
New York, NY 10003

Printed in the United States of America

Library of Congress Cataloging-in-Publication Data

Adams, Carol J.
  Meditations on the inner art of vegetarianism : spiritual practices for
body and soul / Carol J. Adams
      p. cm.
  Includes index.
  ISBN 1-930051-37-9 (alk. paper)
  1. Vegetarianism—Religious aspects. I. Title

BL65 .V44 A34 2001
291.5'693—dc21

2001029779

In honor of
Virginia Louise Buchanan
and in memory of
Arthur Eugene Buchanan,
with deep gratitude

You are the peach,
the fruit,
ripening from the energy
you can bring within yourself.
You are a part of the human soul
orientating itself afresh.
You are not dead to yourself.
You are alive, so abundantly alive!
If you did not know it, the peach tells you so.

Acknowledgments ✿

I am extremely grateful to Martin Rowe who envisioned this book and its possibilities. Enthusiastic thanks to Martin, Mia MacDonald, and Carol Mai for their thoughts on the daily unfolding of the inner art. My abiding gratitude to Pamela Nelson for "Sonic Fruit" and the interconnections it telegraphs and to Kate Sartor Hilburn for her photograph of peaches from her "Fruits of the Spirit" series. And Bruce Buchanan, as always, for his inner art of presence and support.

My recent book, *The Inner Art of Vegetarianism,* celebrates my discovery that vegetarianism had deepened my spirituality. I wanted to express this joy and invite others into the process. The nature of an inner art, I suggested in the book, is that it simultaneously has the feeling of being both necessity and spontaneity. When we develop what I call "the habit of vegetarianism" we discover this nature—a vegetarianism in which what has been willed becomes so necessary to who we are that it has the fresh feeling of both necessity and spontaneity. An inner art is a living, glowing aspect of ourselves, constantly transforming us as we extend its presence in our lives.

In this book of meditations, I offer daily reflections that try to keep the dynamic of necessity and spontaneity alive. If these meditations were seen as answering a question, that question might be, "How do we bring something new into our lives or deepen that which is already a part of us to discover the spirituality in our lives and in our being or becoming a vegetarian?" The inner art occurs when we find ways to bring the energy that wants to change into our day. We learn the art of enlisting the part of us that doesn't want to change into the process of changing.

The same process is at work in vegetarianism as in other spiritual practices. Meditation is the practice of the art of nonattachment; the inner art of vegetarianism enlists meditation to bring centeredness and consciousness to an eating practice. Keeping a journal is the practice of valuing the self-examined life; the inner art of vegetarianism enlists journaling to enable us to develop the skills for self-examined meals. Prayer is a conversation with God or the divine; the inner art of vegetarianism brings animals and plants into this conversation. We pray with our hands as we prepare, serve, and eat healthy vegetarian meals. Dreamwork engages with an aspect of ourselves that is not readily accessible to our conscious self; the inner art of vegetarianism assumes dreams can guide us in changing. Activism is the practice of actively working against injustice; the inner art of vegetarianism recognizes the value of individual efforts at boycotting products derived from the suffering of others.

We can each discover—or unfold—the inner art. The purpose of this meditation book is to provide reflections and prompts that aid us in doing so—that is, assist us in aligning consciousness and action. Ways to enhance your work with this book include:

- Work with one a day. It is your choice how you work: randomly or day by day.

- Read each entry multiple times. Be quiet and intuitive or respond intellectually. Vary the position you are in as you read it.

- Put the book down, close your eyes and follow your inner responses.

- Use your whole body—allow yourself to feel deeply and respect what you are feeling.

- Begin to keep a journal and respond to the meditations in your journal. See where the thoughts on these pages take you in your pages.

Each of you approaches the issues of vegetarianism and spiritual practice from different perspectives and stages in your journey. Because of these varying perspectives, I have tried to separate the daily entries into themes. As a result, the daily entries may be approached either *thematically* or *consecutively*. If you choose to work thematically, you will be able to concentrate on those facets of your spiritual and vegetarian path that call most immediately for your attention. If you choose to work consecutively, a daily unfolding of possibilities is available to you.

Because many of the themes in the inner art of vegetarianism are interwoven, if you do choose to work thematically, I highly recommend that you not just stick to one theme throughout the year. You will, hopefully, find much that is of value to you in other sections. If, however, you do wish to follow the sections, you may refer to the index at the back of the book. The sections are as follows:

Vegetarianism as a Spiritual Practice

Many people—both vegetarians and non-vegetarians—might be surprised at calling vegetarianism a spiritual practice. But, in that it calls us to become aware of our choices, what we put in our bodies, and our relationship to the world around us, vegetarianism possesses all the qualities necessary to form a spiritual practice.

Becoming a Vegetarian

For those thinking of becoming a vegetarian, or finding it hard to continue as a vegetarian, or who wish to re-invigorate their vegetarianism, these meditations offer loving and reflective steps for doing all three.

Fostering Attention

All spiritual practices require discipline. These meditations help us focus on what needs to be changed, cultivated, explored, or nurtured if we are to make the changes we desire that enable us to live with integrity.

The Spiritual Path

These meditations provide a glimpse into what the spiritual path might hold for you, and what kind of transformation might be awaiting you.

Touching the Process

I believe that the best way to begin a spiritual practice is simply to start doing it. These meditations offer insights into how to begin your practice.

Taking the Next Step

Sometimes we become blocked by fears, inertia, or ignorance as to what we have to do to change or keep on growing. These meditations can help move us on to the next step—all the while recognizing that we don't have to know every step of the journey, just the next step.

Growing Roots

One way to cultivate a spiritual practice, especially the practice of vegetarianism, is to acknowledge our connections with the earth and the world around us. These meditations honor our being a part of nature and not apart from nature.

Opening Our Hearts to Other Animals

Many people are disturbed by the cruelty to animals inherent in eating meat. These meditations help us recognize our kinship with other animals, thereby deepening and reorienting our relationships with them.

Cultivating Compassion

Many of us drive ourselves too hard in our quest. Many of us find it hard to open our hearts to others. These meditations reflect on how vegetarianism and spiritual practices enable us to become more compassionate, not only to other human and nonhuman beings, but also to ourselves.

On Dragging the Stone and Pulling on Rice

One of the features of daily life is the way we make things hard on ourselves. We do things that work against our best interests and we don't follow our natural instincts. A spiritual practice offers insights into these unloving ways of relating to ourselves. These two sections reflect on two stories that address honoring our impulses and following a natural path.

Keeping a Journal, The Power of Breath, and Working with Our Dreams

Three fundamental features of spiritual practices, I believe, are keeping a journal to record our feelings and thoughts, working with our dreams, and learning how to breathe properly and consciously. These sections form a brief guide to cultivating these disciplines.

The Vegetarian Cook and A Meditation on Sourdough

Of course, being a vegetarian is necessarily about food—and cooking plays a central role in eating! These meditations explore the sensuous joys of cooking and how using sourdough cultures is a perfect and practical metaphor of the spiritual process at work.

The following reflections draw on various spiritual practices to deepen consciousness, to focus action, and to find a balance between necessity and spontaneity. In this way, we may each discover how vegetarianism awakens us to or deepens our spirituality. I wish you a day-by-day experience of ripening to life and living. You are the peach. You are alive, so abundantly alive! Let each day tell you so.

Happy New World!

Each new year, each new day, invites us into the process of change. Each new year, each new day invites us into a process of self-discovery. This new year, this new day provides an opportunity for expanding your self. We can change the way we experience the world and ourselves in it.

Through vegetarianism, you have the chance to engage in the process of healing the broken heart within and healing the broken world without. Vegetarianism is not so much a diet as an acknowledgment of relationships: between your choice of food and your body's health; between yourself and your sisters and brothers, the animals; and between your actions and the earth's health.

The world is organized to keep you a meat eater, to keep you from acknowledging relationships. Your next step may be to reorganize your world.

Today, ask yourself: What part of my world do I need to reorganize to move forward on my path?

Vegetarianism teaches the gentle yet profound process of change.

Reorienting your life, deepening your spirituality, or exploring or expanding your vegetarianism does not require some absolute conversion experience, though this is possible. It can be a gradual and liberating unfolding, one step following another. One day at a time, one meal at a time.

Identify one thing you can change about your life today—no matter how small it may seem—and do it.

The process of spiritual practice, in the beginning, is a
process of opening oneself up.

There is no one way to become a vegetarian, but there are many possible vegetarians within you—a vegetarian concerned about animals, a vegetarian concerned about the environment, a vegetarian concerned about the health of one's body, a vegetarian concerned about suffering. Through the spiritual practice of vegetarianism, you access and honor these possible vegetarians.

You open yourself up to the possibility that you can *respond* to suffering, not ignore it; that you can *care* about your own health, not postpone caring; that you can be *engaged* with the world.

What is the most important change you want for the world? Ask yourself, am I helping this change happen? If so, give thanks for those actions. If not, identify what you need to do.

*As with any other spiritual practice, vegetarianism
begins with attention and discipline and evolves into a
habit that feels natural.*

Vegetarians bring attention to the process of choosing food. We remember; we don't just react. We make connections; we don't just consume. Vegetarians enact the same insights that arise during meditation—that all beings are interconnected. Vegetarianism is meditation in action.

**Think of five words that describe what you want
from a spiritual practice.**

> *The inner art of vegetarianism is a sanctuary in a world*
> *of suffering.*

The outer world is often one of suffering, exploitation, and thoughtlessness. As an individual, that world may alarm you. As an activist, you challenge it. As a vegetarian, you know that with each meal you reject that world, and instead create a sanctuary that supports your sense that the world can be otherwise—loving, thoughtful, and nonviolent.

List your favorite vegetarian foods.

Each of us desires wholeness.

The inner art of vegetarianism—the practice of living from a diet composed wholly of vegetables, grains, fruits, nuts, and seeds—arises from a desire for wholeness. Wholeness is a process, not a product. Wholeness unfolds through spiritual practice. Vegetarianism is a spiritual practice that mirrors wholeness in its meal.

Fix a vegetarian meal and as you prepare the vegetables ask yourself: How have I felt fragmented in my life? How can food function to affirm a feeling of wholeness?

Our wholeness is tied to the rest of creation.

We value wholeness in our food; we resist separation and divided consciousness. This wholeness invites us to bring wholeness even more fully into our lives. We learn this by being honest about our needs. And we learn how to be honest about ourselves through spiritual practice.

Write a letter to yourself about your spiritual quest and desires and put it away to be read in a year's time.

To talk about spirituality is to talk about energy.

The spiritual path consists of understanding how we channel our energy and where or why we block it. Our spiritual task is to understand the quality of the energy and find out where it wants to go. We manifest energy or we can block it.

Ask yourself: What is most interesting and crucial for my body this moment?

The inner art of vegetarianism is a tangible spiritual practice.

Because you eat, your day helps to shape it; if you have made the commitment to it, your day pulls you forward into it. While other practices may be skipped for a day or more, eating is a necessity that, unless you are fasting, happens more than once a day. Uniting a practice with a necessity catalyzes the process of becoming aware of things, or intentionality. It catalyzes it because if you choose to be intentional you are given, at least three times a day, the opportunity to enact and experience intentionality.

Practice listening to others today—friends, strangers, the wind, the trees, animals.

Our relationships with animals touch a very deep place
within ourselves.

When we close off our relationship with that very deep
place—either because it is too painful to go near or because we
don't give it the time—we are closing off the possibility of
wholeness for ourselves. If we eat meat, we may close off our
relationship with that deep place, and may not be able to go
near it because doing so would mean we would have to
become aware of what we do to animals. Vegetarians learn how
to access that deep place and honor it.

Think about an animal who has been important
in your life.

We are each on a spiritual path.

Even though we may feel confused or alienated, even though we may be so deeply consumed by living that we have not recognized the spirituality in our actions, we are on a spiritual path. We may be on a spiritual path and not know how to balance the demands of the "real" world with our own inner needs. We may be firmly settled into a spiritual practice and yet resisting some aspects of change—perhaps vegetarianism. Our spiritual path may be to enliven a vegetarianism that we now take for granted. It may be to learn to articulate connections we enact. Our spiritual path requires our attention.

Take a winter forest walk and listen for pinecones popping.

Attention is awareness that awakens us to meaning in our actions.

The night before I became a vegetarian, I went out to dinner with my mother and a friend at a fancy steak house in Cambridge, Massachusetts. Being sentimental, I was saying my goodbyes to my identity as a meat eater. I was going to eat my last meal of meat conscious of my choice to be eating meat. As I looked at the steak, I was aware that this was the last time I'd be eating a steak. In thinking that, my mind immediately asked me why I was even eating this steak. Internally, I had begun to shift to vegetarianism because I was bringing attention to my eating habits. This attention then required some investigation of my choices.

Buy a few condolence cards for people whose companion animals have died. Use them throughout the year when appropriate and necessary.

> *The gift that vegetarianism offers is that we can follow*
> *the process of awareness and not cut it off when we*
> *discover what is happening to animals on this planet.*

We do not have to hide from disturbing information about the suffering of animals. We do not have to split ourselves in two. By following the process of awareness, we are made whole.

What do you know about animals' lives? Reflect on the positive and negative things that are happening to animals. Pay special attention to those aspects in which your life intersects with the lives of animals.

Spiritual practice is the act of bringing attention to our lives.

Each moment we have the possibility of being attentive to our lives or the lives of others. Each moment we face the possibility that we might not be attentive to our lives and the lives of others. The element that differentiates acting with attention from acting without attention is practice. We need to ask ourselves: How much practice have we had acting with attention? How much practice have we had acting without it? If we can bring attention to how we move, eat, breathe, or feel, we can bring attention to other aspects of our lives. If we have not brought attention to *any aspect* of our lives, it is difficult to bring it to *specific* aspects of our lives.

Identify something you rushed through in the past day or two. Can you return to it with attention? Can you perform the task with awareness?

---

*Vegetarians have already cultivated the basic quality
that can help them change or grow: They are already
attentive.*

When we bring attention to our eating practice, we place
attention between what we see and what we eat. We don't
accept the category "Food" as we have been conditioned to
view it. At first, when I became a vegetarian and was offered
meat, I became aware of my attention, which announced,
"This is not meat, this is a dead animal." Such conscious
placement of attention was necessary as I crossed over from
one identity to another.

It reminded me that there was meaning attached to eating
meat—a meaning that was disturbing. I did not want to eat
meat. Attention helped me to act consistent with that desire.

**Include an animal activist group in the list of
charities you support. If you already support one
or more, add another. Read their mailings.**

*Each day I have the opportunity to live with attention
or inattention.*

When I live with attention, I can follow my awareness. If
my awareness reminds me that "meat is from a dead animal,"
I can engage with this fact about my food and allow this
engagement to change me. When I chose inattentiveness, I
cannot let awareness work within me. I must use my energy to
block it.

**What does it feel like to live in your body at this
moment? What does it feel like to bring attention
to your body?**

We can learn as much from when we neglect to be attentive as when we are attentive.

We can learn as much from when we neglect to be attentive as when we are attentive—as long as we become attentive to our inattention! Being inattentive is a choice. As long as we acknowledge we are making choices, and that these choices at times lead us away from being attentive, we continue to grow in awareness. We become aware of our desire *not* to be aware. But in this, we are learning how to cultivate attention.

Today, I will bring attention to the act of choosing food.

> *Spiritual practice includes the invisible within our daily
> schedule.*

Vegetarians affirm the invisible world. They acknowledge
the hidden world where animals are alive and aren't just bodies
processing plant protein for us. Animals have qualities that
may seem invisible to us—consciousness and how they
experience life. Vegetarians affirm these aspects of animals'
lives. We don't have to see each animal to acknowledge each
one's uniqueness.

We vegetarians not only believe in the invisible, we hold
on to the invisible in the presence of sensuous temptations of
the visible, the smells, tastes, memories, and demands on our
time and conscience. To be committed to the spiritual life is to
say, "I believe in the invisible world." To be committed to a
vegetarian life is to say, "I believe I am connected to all
animals. They may be invisible to me, but I will include them
in my daily practice."

**Take time to go within. Say a prayer or meditate
today.**

"What shall I do with my day?"

You may be following a spiritual path within a specific religious tradition, or perhaps you are not. Whether you are inside or outside an organized religion, one way to think about spirituality is that it addresses the question, "What shall I do with my life?" Spirituality answers that question. It answers the question, "What shall I do with my day?" Even more specifically, it answers the question, "What am I doing now?"

Ask yourself, "What shall I do with my day?" Answer it with the idea that you actually have a choice. Then consider: Where does your energy wish to go?

> *How each of us responds to vegetarian consciousness is*
> *part of our spiritual path.*

Within the context of the very direct question, "What shall I do with my life?", vegetarian spirituality asks, "What shall I do with this consciousness about vegetarianism? Do I incorporate it into my life or do I ignore it? Will I chose attention or inattention? Will I manifest vegetarian energy or will I block it?"

Assess your pantry: From soups to prepared guacamole, you can stock what you will need when you want to eat so that you can eat with attention.

> *"What shall I do with this consciousness about vegetarianism?"*

In answering the questions, "What shall I do with this consciousness about vegetarianism? Do I incorporate it into my life or do I ignore it?", we have to understand our unconscious as well as conscious desires. Often we move through a day without attentiveness to the drives that are determining so much of the day. Unconscious patterns are present in unexamined activities. An unexamined activity is in some way "dead"—we move through it without awareness. We do it, but it does not touch us. We bring no "life" to it, no consciousness. Consciousness and action become one when we bring the unconscious patterns that influence our actions to consciousness, examine them, and determine whether or not they are in tune with what we want to do with our lives, our days, our moments.

Plan to prepare an easy vegan meal or order a cheeseless vegetarian pizza.

The inner art of vegetarianism acknowledges the interconnectedness of all beings and enacts compassion toward them.

It acts on the understanding that we express ourselves through relationships and that these relationships include the other animals.

We make the following promise to all animals, those who are eaten, those used to produce milk and eggs, and honeybees: I will not take from you or fragment you to feed myself. The inner art of vegetarianism, therefore, is a commitment to a diet that is animal-free so that animals may be free.

Order a catalog from a company, like Pangea, that sells products not made out of animals.

*The archetypal psychologist James Hillman observes,
"Demands ask fulfillment, needs require only
expression."*

We all have needs. We make some of our needs conscious
and act on them. We keep some of our needs unconscious and
yet still act on them. And, for a variety of reasons, we keep
some of our needs so tightly under wraps that they are not
acted on or acknowledged. These needs require expression but
instead experience repression. When we desire to change
something about our lives, these needs may be lying there
unacknowledged. If we realize that we are, in fact, not
changing—though we will ourselves to do so—that stagnation
may be because our needs require expression.

**Meditate on the quality you would like to have
more of in your life. Repeat this meditation.
Envision the quality as a part of you.**

Our needs reveal where the wild things are.

In his famous children's book, *Where the Wild Things Are*, Maurice Sendak depicts a young boy who has been sent to his room. A tree and an ocean and a boat appear, and he travels to where the Wild Things are. The Wild Things are marvelous, big beings. When someone asked Sendak how he knew these wild things would not scare little children, he replied, "Because they do not scare me." He knew himself that well. The wild things of your unconscious need not scare you. You can recognize them for what they are—a part of your spiritual path. They are your needs that require expression.

For fifteen minutes write a list that begins, "I want…" What do you discover?

Our inner wild things are unvalued.

A sense of unworthiness may be the motivation for staying hooked to the demands of the outer world and ignoring our inner wild things. When we measure ourselves through what we produce rather than through who we are, our inner wild thing may become more frantic.

Inner wild thing: I'm here. Please shed some light on me.

The mind: I can't! I'm too busy. There's a lot to do. You seem to be fine in there. There is so much need. You don't need anything.

Inner wild thing: I do! I need nurturing. I need some help. There's a lot we could be doing. But I need you.

The mind: Sorry. Another time.

Rewrite this dialogue to give attention to your inner wild thing.

We may neglect our inner wild things because we are ashamed of having needs.

Inner wild thing: Wait! You need this too. Your jealousy, needs, frustrations—where do you think they are coming from? From me. As long as you don't attend to me, my frustrations are powerful. But even more powerful is when I am released. I don't like being this small, this ignored. I have needs too.

The mind: I am ashamed of needs. I am ashamed of these needs. I don't want to be needy.

Inner wild thing: Ignoring me makes you more needy. Be honest with yourself. That is your need. We are all worthy of this.

Affirm to yourself: I am worthy of this. I am worthy of this time.

> *For change to happen we have to be conscious of our*
> *choices and then consciously change our choices.*

As we make our choices conscious, we may begin to realize how what we are doing in our lives helps us cope with needs we may never have articulated. We then have to step back and recognize something revolutionary in this culture of instant gratification: We don't have to fulfill our needs, we only need to express them. This means we can acknowledge our needs without necessarily always acting upon them.

Give something away today.

*Developing the art of balancing the needy and visionary
parts of oneself is a spiritual practice.*

Nonvegetarians are often aware they are eating an animal who was killed for them, and then stop that thought, "I don't want to think about that right now." The needy part, desirous to eat that meat—or so it thinks— overwhelms the visionary part, desirous of a humane diet. This means that a dissonance in spirit, mind, and body exists. Nonvegetarians cannot allow the process of vegetarian awareness to touch them, because a part of them resists change.

Reflect on how to accept the gift of vegetarian consciousness, "Today, I will accept the gift of vegetarian consciousness by...."

Once we recognize that needs do not demand fulfillment, the challenge becomes to live with that insight.

When we can live with the insight that our needs do not require fulfillment, we have moved one step closer to changing the habits that keep us from cultivating habits that allow for growth. We do this by entering willingly into dialogue with both our needy part and our visionary part. We learn to listen to our *needy* part so that it does not sabotage the *visionary* part.

For ten minutes, write with your nondominant hand. If you need a focus for this writing exercise, ask yourself, "What are my needs?"

To continue without inner work is to miss the true and deep self.

The tragedy of the unfulfilled life is that it is a life that could not encounter the true self. Instead, it settled for living with confusion, superficiality, and lack of clarity. It feared the wild things rather than allowing them expression.

Turn off the television for today.

Spiritual practices provide a bridge to the unconscious aspects of our lives, and allow us to integrate them.

Spiritual practices awaken or enliven our daily lives. Often when we are blocked—blocked from becoming vegetarians or beginning or extending a spiritual practice—it is because our mind and our body are not communicating with each other. To unblock ourselves we have to learn to receive our unconscious concerns and issues.

Act on an intuitive feeling today.

*Often our responses teach us how great the distance is
between consciousness and action.*

In becoming or being a vegetarian you may first learn
from what was resistant to change. And then from not
changing—from this resistance—you can learn how to
change: How to align consciousness and action.

**Dedicate your day to an idea. Every hour try to
bring yourself back to that idea.**

Working with guilt can be transformative.

First, you are aware that you feel guilty.

Secondly, you reflect on this. What is causing my guilt? What is it telling me about my behavior? Should I change my behavior and/or compensate for my behavior?

Thirdly, you act. You use your guilt to inform yourself, and then you align your behavior with your consciousness. Guilt can teach us about our own deep need to unite consciousness and action.

Make way for the new: Clean out your closet.

The process of being grounded creates the ability to change.

To cultivate a spiritual practice, we deepen ourselves. We sink into ourselves and find refuge there. In deepening, we meet the universe at a more profound level. We turn ourselves inside out and discover the universe within. We encounter the goodness that resides within ourselves and experience the goodness in the universe.

This is the process of grounding. Being grounded is one of the results of following a spiritual practice. It is also one of my definitions of vegetarianism.

List the ways you become grounded.

I am flesh; I am of the Earth; whence we come, to which
we return.

The word "Human" comes from the Indo-European root
word *dhghem-*, meaning "Earth." From this root word we get
the word "Humus," the soil.

(Dh)ghom-on– means "Earthling." Yoga, meditation,
vegetarianism, dreamwork, and keeping a journal are spiritual
practices that offer grounding: You are flesh. You are of the
earth. You are an earthling. You can come to ground. You can
come home to the Earth.

Notice the world outside your window.

You can change the energy flow of your earthling body.

Bonnie Bainbridge Cohen observes that, while we cannot see the wind, we can see where the wind has passed in the patterns on the sand. In the same way, we reveal where our energy has been through our body. A body worker would discover a different history for you than a traditional biographer would uncover; the biographer has the writing in the sand, the body worker the writing on the body. You may not be able to change your biography, but you can change the energy flow of your earthling body. You can come home to it.

How can you be more comfortable in your body today?

It is easier to grow when one has roots.

When you feel rooted in something, you feel at home and empowered, and act from a sense of abundance rather than from a sense of loss or limitation. When you are grounded you can relate to the world as continuous with you, connected to you through that grounding.

Take a walk and feel thankfulness for the world you encounter.

The more grounded one becomes in a practice, the easier it is to bring it to other parts of one's life.

When you are not grounded, you feel separate from the world and alienated from yourself. At such times, you are unstable ground. Then you cause mountain slides and avalanches.

Take a moment during the day to plant your feet firmly on the ground. Feel what it is like to be grounded.

When we are grounded, we can grow.

Just as yoga practice extends you (people often literally grow because yoga practice allows the spine to extend), spiritual practice helps you grow. You are being stretched. You try new things. You can be more empathetic, more flexible in spirit. You can reach out.

Lift your arms above your head and stretch. Feel your spine lengthening.

*If we can find it within ourselves to love our bodies, why
not the bodies of others?*

When we take time to acknowledge the intricate ways in
which our bodies function, we may develop a way to
acknowledge the intricate ways in which the bodies of others
function. This can deepen our vegetarianism or contribute to
a movement toward vegetarianism. The more aware we are of
our own bodies, the more sympathy we can cultivate for others
with bodies, including the other animals.

**Ask yourself the key question: what is most
interesting or crucial for me this moment?**

Because of vegetarianism, you can encounter your inner
self.

Through the inner art of vegetarianism you can integrate thought, belief, commitment, and practice. It ignites a positive energy that frees you to experience the world in a new way. It can lead you in directions you didn't know you would go. Indeed, without it you might not have known how to go. Because of vegetarianism, you will probably become a better cook. Because of vegetarianism, you can encounter your inner self—you have something within to nurture.

Enjoy a moment of thankful silence before you eat.

Vegetarianism teaches us about integration.

When we integrate something desired, like vegetarianism or another spiritual practice into our lives, we communicate with that part of the self that desires wholeness. In integrating, we create an internal shift. We open an inner door and reveal that there is more to the self than we had thought. We discover inner resources we didn't know we had. It has been vegetarianism that taught me that. It can teach you as well.

Commit to something today—just today. Try to maintain the commitment throughout the day.

Integration is related to integrity.

Integrity is a quality or commitment an individual can bring to her or his life. It is an awareness about how to live with commitment and honesty, honoring one's own best impulses. Integration is the conscious application of energy. Integration, then, is a key component of spiritual practice. Practice helps us integrate awareness with action.

Today think about how you can integrate different parts of yourself.

> *In my hand I hold a source of creativity, a decision-maker, an objective ally, my best friend, and the silent partner of all my efforts. It is my journal.*

In your journal, you can express feelings, trust yourself, and track your forward and backward movement. Keeping a journal lets the soul speak, not in a linear fashion, but circular and spiraling. It helps you become authentic. Let your journal be your friend, your confidant, your healer, your objective ally, and your silent partner.

Select a notebook for your journal. Write something in it. Don't try to be literary or clever, unless you want to be! Just write what you like. But, write!

In starting a journal you make a promise to yourself; by writing in it you keep that promise.

Keeping a journal is an act of loving yourself—you send yourself a daily valentine. Rereading it, you encounter that love and open the valentine.

Can you take the time to write about what you are feeling and thinking today?

*If we need another's pain for our own gratification, we
generally avoid knowledge about what he or she is
feeling.*

In this situation, it's what *we* are feeling that is
important—that and that alone. Out of our wounded natures,
we place ourselves at the top of the pyramid and through
relationships of power inflict pain, or allow others to inflict
pain, in order to meet our needs. Complex feelings about our
relationship to animals are closed off so we don't have to
process or encounter our own actions for or against animals.
Once we bring attention to the lives of individual animals, we
can ask about the nature of those lives. If the animals are
suffering, we bring attention to our role in their suffering.

**Place yourself in the position of an animal
confined in a factory farm. How does it make you
feel?**

We cannot be bystanders to violence, we must bear witness against violence.

Judith Herman in a brilliant book on violence and its aftermath, *Trauma and Recovery*, writes, "All the perpetrator asks is that the bystander do nothing. He appeals to the universal desire to see, hear, and speak no evil. The victim, on the contrary, asks the bystander to share the burden of pain. The victim demands action, engagement, and remembering." In the face of violence there is no such thing as neutrality. What poses as neutrality is apathy, and apathy sides with the one doing violence. This is why caring is intensively active.

Are you a part of a faith community? Ask them to pray for domesticated animals.

Animals are victims of violence. They ask for
engagement.

There are in fact no bystanders to meat eating. We are
either complicit in or resistant to violence. Violence says, "Let
me put my foot on your neck." The bystander says not only,
"You have a foot on your neck," but also "My, aren't you tasty
with that foot on your neck?" "My, how good violence tastes!"
The loving one says, "Let's get that foot off your neck."

**Reflect on the meaning of nonviolence. What
does that word conjure up for you?**

We have before us two choices: the choice of violence or love.

Violence says, "I need your pain."

The loving one says, "I care that you are suffering and I want to help stop it."

Love is being able to ask what others are going through and allow ourselves to imagine what a pig or a cow or a chicken would answer if we could hear them. And then, because we love them and ourselves enough, we would take our feet off their necks.

Go to your local health food store and inquire about an unfamiliar vegan food.

A spiritual person allows for flow rather than control in her or his life.

Flow and control are the opposite of each other. The problem is that control has a hook—it's easier, simpler, more "real," more tangible. It's got history on its side. By fostering attention, you are able to differentiate between what awareness requires of you and what control enforces upon you. The payoff for staying connected to control is more immediate, but so are the frustrations. A spiritual practice is about flow; it is not about control.

Spiritual practices create inner openness. This inner openness enables the adoption of vegetarianism. One flows toward it.

Identify a hunch you followed successfully.

*Your judging mind reacts first and shows you through its
resistance where you have to go.*

There is a pattern to growth that includes resistance. Your
mind may lead the way by announcing, "I would never do
that." And your conscious self believes this to be true. After all,
it is a common enough thought: It establishes boundaries, it
damns as it dams energy flow. Whenever you find yourself
saying "I'll never do that" or "I could never do that!", it may
be a sign that you are being led towards that which you think
you could never do. The intensity of the reaction is your clue.

**Is something new available to you? Try
responding with "I'll try" rather than "I won't" or
"I can't."**

Taking the next step is following the flow of energy.

When we encounter something new we are often resistant. Yet, our first reaction—"I will not encounter you. I will not change"—can become welcoming, "I want to let you into my life." Before long, if you follow the flow, what you thought was too hard, or too difficult, too impossible or too unattainable, is exactly where you need to be.

When was the last time you said, "I could never do that" in response to something that could be positive in your life? What was it in response to? What specific act could you do in line with this? Can you do it now? Do it. If not, why not?

Vegetarian cooking as meditation says "I am awake!" as I cook.

Vegetarian cooking as meditation announces, "I'm connected to the process of growth. I'm connected to this food, to the people who harvested it, to those with whom I share it, to all unseen but cherished animals."

Put your apron on and say to yourself, "I am committed to this time and space, this cooking experience. I will be here now. Here, in this kitchen, with this food, in this moment."

We are turning from transcendence to immanence.

As children we live in a world of immanence—where everything is connected to us, the world is alive, and animals are present to us in stories and dreams and as helpers. Then we move into relationships based on transcendence—of being separate from, and often above, the world and its beings, whether human or not.

Part of the reason why we grow spiritually may be that we set our sights on something, achieve it, but find we are still not satisfied. So, we either set our heights even higher, and further a transcendence model, or we pause and say, "There has to be something else." If we do the latter, we are turning from transcendence to immanence. Vegetarianism is one way to do this.

Spend a day hibernating. What does it mean to allow the body to sleep and shut down?

Vegetarian spirituality grows from self-acceptance.

Vegetarianism need not be a "should" imposed by the inner judge, but an expression of the love we bring to ourselves. We experience an abundance within, and we can bring it out—not because someone expects us to, or because it is another step on the escalator of success, but because our inner sense of self finds its completion from embracing through love, touching the world, healing and repairing it in our daily actions.

Develop your own rituals of healing and repairing the world.

The process of lovingly adopting vegetarianism is like the process of apple juice settling.

Nonvegetarians think vegetarianism involves a battle with the body. It doesn't. Our body can lead us forward. The Vietnamese Buddhist monk Thich Nhat Hanh describes a glass of freshly poured apple juice. The floating sediments in the juice cause it to look cloudy. When the sediments have settled to the bottom, the apple juice looks clear. The process of lovingly adopting vegetarianism is the process of the apple juice settling. It happens. We become clearer.

Enjoy a luxurious glass of apple or another fruit juice. Savor every sip.

A spiritual person enables a new perspective on feelings.

A spiritual person understands that our feelings need not frighten or confuse us. You don't need to judge emotions, only be aware of them. You realize that unwanted emotions are not bad, they are simply unwanted. Not having to dominate your feelings allows you to experience connections. Once feelings are able to be encountered, then you can be in touch with your feelings about animals. You don't have to protest to yourself or others, "I don't want to know." You can receive your feelings. You can let love grow within. Your capacity to care is increased, not controlled.

Tonight, write down a few sentences about your day. What were you feeling?

Live in the moment.

Don't worry about what you didn't accomplish yesterday or what you need to be doing tomorrow. Accept the gift of this moment. There is a point in trying this. The present will reveal that point to you.

Show gratitude to yourself, "I am attempting something wonderful but difficult. I appreciate myself for trying. I will live in this moment."

*Each time we shop for living food, we are in tune with
a rhythm of life.*

We use our senses to choose the vegetables we will prepare
for our meal. We use sight and touch and smell. We lift, we
look, we smell, we touch, we choose, or we put down. We
choose the eggplant by its size, color, and shape. Is it firm and
smooth? Is it wrinkled anywhere? Are the leaves of the brussels
sprouts wilted? Does the broccoli smell cabbagy? Choose
another. Look at the chard. Is it crisp and fresh?

Each time we shop, we lift, we look, we smell, we touch,
we choose. We are in tune with a rhythm of life.

**Go to the store and touch different vegetables.
What do you notice?**

We are not so much a single "I" as a multiplicity of selves.

We aren't unchangeable, although a part of us might be. We are a mixture of selves—those that want to change and those that don't. Often, rather than engage with some aspect of these selves, we actively work to deny them a hearing. Through dialogue with those parts of ourselves that don't want to change, we can engage and learn from that part that we are denying.

Dialogue makes conscious those internal conversations and unexamined assumptions we have about ourselves. It allows our selves to be in conversation with each other, rather than working against each other. Dialogue is particularly present when we are in the process of changing. We ask ourselves, "Will this work?"

In your journal, ask and answer: What do I want? Do I want to remain who I have always been or do I want to change?

We can empty ourselves of past identities and become who we need to be.

Between birth and death, between coming from our mothers and returning to the Earth, we are each in the process of creation and recreation. Our skin, alone, replaces itself every twenty-seven days. We are free, free to adapt and free to change. The revelation occurs when we say to ourselves, "I have always done it this way, but I don't need to."

During the day, repeat to yourself, "I have always done it this way, but I don't need to." How do you feel saying this and hearing this?

Developing a spiritual practice is participating in the act of creation.

When someone who is a nonvegetarian becomes a vegetarian, she or he has created something new: A vegetarian self. When someone who does not meditate becomes a meditator, she or he, too, has created something new: A meditating self. In adopting a yoga practice, an individual creates something new: A yogini or yogin. When we bring something new into our lives, when we cultivate a spiritual practice, we participate in the act of creation.

Light a candle and make an intention for this day: What is it you intend to create?

Advice to writers is advice for anyone on the path of creation.

The mechanism of creating may be different, but the process is the same: To become a writer, you must be gentle with yourself, but firm with your expectations and your rituals. To succeed as a writer, you must come to the paper and be at your station. Be aware of your expectations: You cannot come and write the complete book simply and directly. What will happen when you start writing will influence you and draw you in. You don't have to know how the book will end; you only need to bring yourself to the process of writing.

Just so with a spiritual practice. Forgive yourself your stumbles, but be firm with your expectations and rituals.

Write a poem, a list, or a letter, to express gratitude. Address it to the Creator or the Earth.

Let your senses smell, taste, touch, and see and in so doing speak to your inner self.

The materials you need for the spiritual process are different from those of a writer, but you keep coming back to them. If it is vegetarianism, your materials are legumes, grains, vegetables, herbs, fruits, tofu, seitan, tempeh. Handle them. Smell them. Try them in different ways. You'll find that your diet will expand. Let your senses smell, taste, touch, and see and in so doing speak to your inner self. It is not only your diet that you are changing. You have the marvelous opportunity to discover this fact.

Draw your favorite vegetable in the way you desire—simple or detailed, abstract or realistic. Enjoy the act of drawing and the act of looking at a vegetable.

Vegetarian cooking unites us with creation.

Vegetarian cooking teaches us about the process of creativity. We experience how it feels to bring something new into existence without taking something out of existence. We can take that experience of creating something new into other parts of our life.

Read through a vegetarian cookbook and envision yourself cooking.

We need different skills creating a new habit than we do maintaining it.

The Buddha said, "One need not carry the raft on one's head after crossing the stream." The energy needed to cross the stream is different from the energy we need once we are on the other side. That is because the methods we use to bring something new into our lives will be different from the methods we use to maintain a spiritual practice.

Write down your favorite vegetarian saying and place it on your refrigerator.

We have to use the material available to us to raft across
the river.

The materials needed to cross the river are time and the quality of our attention. Attention is the way in which we focus our energy, time is the way we experience the gift of being embodied, and rafting is the process of change that time and attention enable. We discover the current in the river that pulls us across.

Where in your house do you feel calm, centered, aware, at peace? Can you spend a few minutes there today?

When you are crossing the stream from a nonpractice to practice, time is your raft—it is your lifesaver.

You may ask, "Who has the time to go rafting?" Time is the one thing we do have. To bring a practice into your life successfully has a great deal to do with how you view time. Take the time! You are worth the time it takes to create a practice.

At the next big rainstorm, look at a stream, a lake or river and see how it has changed.

Time requires us to make choices.

Sometimes we prefer to be passive about time, something that is fine as long as we recognize that this passivity is a choice. And this choice often prevents us from cultivating a relationship with our inner self. At first, everything to which we commit requires time. Passivity need not be our only choice.

Set a time today to meet your inner self.

Start with your big toe.

A story is told about Moses and the parting of the Red Sea so that the Hebrew people could escape from slavery and into the Promised Land. It is said that the waters did not part until Moses put his big toe into them. The journey to vegetarianism or another spiritual practice—from a form of captivity to old habits and cultural conditioning to liberation—requires that we put our big toe into the waters.

Use some lotion or oil and massage your big toes and then both feet. You never know where they might take you.

A spiritual person identifies the next step and takes it.

Spirituality is a commitment to live deeply enough within yourself to be present to what is happening now and open to what the next step is. It does not require the final step, only the readiness for the next one, and the next. The next step: That is your spiritual path.

Make an appointment with yourself to _____.

You only have to take one step at a time.

Be specific. Say to yourself, "I will not try to do everything. I will not be overwhelmed by the big picture. I will be specific in my choices." This is the art of focusing. It requires taking only one step, not many.

Identify your next step.

"There is no beginning too small."

Naturalist and vegetarian Henry David Thoreau said, "There is no beginning too small." Small beginnings may be necessary when the issue is changing one's food habits because we have so many emotional issues around food. If our mind gets wind of big changes ahead, it may brace every mental nerve and muscle against the change—even though our body may welcome a dramatic change in diet. You don't have to make a cataclysmic change. You can take small steps. There is no beginning too small.

Clean out a kitchen drawer.

If life is in the details, vegetarian cooking is your magnifying glass.

In cooking, we experience the details the world often ignores. What is one-eighth of a teaspoon? One-eighth of a teaspoon of saffron threads or cayenne will give us an answer as it infuses flavor throughout a dish. Our small beginnings may be like one-eighth of a teaspoon of cayenne— transforming.

Use an unfamiliar spice in your cooking today.

> *As with any spiritual practice, becoming a vegetarian*
> *requires keeping promises we make to ourselves.*

Promises represent our hopes for ourselves. Yet keeping a promise can be very difficult. If you break it, no one knows but you. But if you can't keep a promise with yourself, who can you keep it with? You are worth keeping your own promises. What promises have you made to yourself that you have not kept? Can you make a different promise that acts on the desire for wholeness?

Write down as many adjectives as come to mind that describe how you are feeling.

The Seesaw Principle of Time and Practice.

When two children want to play on a seesaw, they first must align the board. If one child weighs more than the other, they move the board so that more of it is on the side of the lighter child. That way the board contributes its weight to the child's and together they come near to equaling the other child's weight. Then the play can begin, and the rhythm of riding up and riding down will be smooth.

Your inner life sits at one end of a seesaw and your outer life—its demands, schedules, and relationships—is at the other end. Time is the board on which they sit. At first, in bringing a new practice into our lives, our inner life is like the lighter child. It requires some compensation from the board to equal the massive outer life that faces it. Time is what we give our inner self. We have to love ourselves enough to wrench out of our schedules the time to learn what our soul longs for for us.

Take the time to look through an old photo album. Be grateful for your memories and reflect on how time has worked in your life.

To create a practice, you need to be aware of your own weaknesses around time.

When we are unfocused, our weaknesses will determine how we spend our time. Without focus, we are more susceptible to allowing others to determine our own agenda. They find a way to appeal to our weakness. "This is a really important meeting." And you hear yourself saying, "Okay I'll go." And then as you sit there at the meeting, you realize that the meeting wasn't all that important and you ask yourself why you allowed yourself to be talked into going.

You need to develop the ability to say that you'll "think about it." When you're under pressure to give an immediate answer, you're less likely to act with your own self in consideration. When you are alone, you can assess: Is this indeed an important meeting or not? If it is, you can still say yes; if it is not, you are able to say, "I am sorry, I can't do that."

Say "no" to something so that you can make room for something important.

Keeping promises to ourselves is a way to say to our unconscious, "I will meet you here."

By keeping our promises, we signal our commitment. The art of doing it is important. By keeping your promise to be a vegetarian for one meal, or one day, or one week, or your life, you send a message to the unconscious that you honor yourself. And in being successful, you get the message you can do it. You have met yourself here. You increase your abilities to actualize your goals because you know, both consciously and unconsciously, that you can indeed establish a next step and take it.

Take fifteen minutes and plan vegetarian meals for your day.

What is within me is equally important as my actions.

Through vegetarian cooking we act on the interconnections that the unconscious senses. It allows us to be alive—to ourselves, the other animals, the Earth, and this moment. Vegetarian cooking as meditation means we bring ourselves to the process of cooking vegetarian food. Paying attention to the act of cooking means that I am in my kitchen, with the foods and the utensils to create, at that very moment, something nourishing and delicious. I step into the process of cooking.

Prepare a salad. Notice: water as it runs off the vegetables; the knife as it slices; the bowl that holds the salad.

In keeping the promise, change happens.

When we keep a promise with ourselves, three things happen interdependently: First, we let our inner self know that we are listening. We say to it, "I will go there. I won't turn away." Second, we unblock and follow the energy that arises from a deeper self rather than from our conditioned self. And third, we connect to the universe of spiritual energy.

Throughout the day, remind yourself, "I am awake!"

A Meditation on the Elements, for the Spring Equinox.

Breathing in, I see myself as flowing water.
Breathing out, I feel fresh.
Breathing in, I see myself as fire.
Breathing out, I feel vibrant.
Breathing in, I see myself as air.
Breathing out, I feel spacious.
Breathing in, I see myself as earth.
Breathing out, I feel grounded.

> **Sit still. If you feel your back slump, sit on a pillow or a chair. As you breathe in, say to yourself, "Breathing in, I see myself as flowing water." As you breathe out, say to yourself, "Breathing out, I feel fresh." After several breaths, when you begin to feel focused, breathe in and say simply, "Flowing water" and breathe out and say simply, "Fresh." This process may last for five minutes or so. When you feel present to yourself, move to the next couplet. Continue through the meditation, devoting about fifteen minutes to it.**

Food prepared with love radiates.

Preparing vegetarian foods, I become aware of feelings of holiness and gentleness—of an integration of the senses without the disintegration of bodies. The quiet affirmation of thyme, rosemary, and garlic in an Italian bread, the tofu baking with hoisin sauce, the savory stuffing. The smells of the food themselves express love.

Open your senses to all the smells, sights, sounds, tastes, and tactile things around you.

Each of us resists change.

What keeps us from taking the first step? Or the next? What halts our best intentions? I grew up reciting a confession I found achingly true as well as beautiful, "We have left undone those things which we ought to have done; and we have done those things which we ought not to have done." The part of us that resists is the part that prefers the way things have always been done. It prefers to do what it has been conditioned to do.

This conditioned mind, this clinging mind, this roaming, flitting, judging, anxious, and impatient mind squeezes out the room to discover any other way of thinking and being. It holds onto the last step.

What did you identify as your next step? What reasons has your conditioned mind given for not taking it?

*From the mind's perspective, there is mind and there is
not mind.*

This is the dualism from which others arise. We enact
these other dualisms in our daily lives. The most basic ones we
cling to are: male/female, human/animal, mind/body,
nature/culture, subject/object. I believe these dualisms have
caused a great deal of human and nonhuman suffering. We are
conditioned to see these dualisms as "facts" rather than as
interpretations—biased interpretations. The mind identifies
with control. There is another way. Spiritual practices allow
the mind to experience nondualism in one's life.

**Try and see yourself from different perspectives
and heights. See yourself from the perspective of
an ant and an elephant.**

The conditioned mind identifies with a constant, unchanging, and independent self.

The conditioned mind is that part of us which is conditioned to believe in and act upon dualism—that convenient way we make divisions of experience and objects into separate and opposite things.

The conditioned mind accepts as true that there is mind and there is body, or mind and soul. It believes its role is to think and, in thinking, to plan, and in planning, to divide.

The conditioned mind thinks we are separate, and sees us as separate selves. In bringing a spiritual practice like vegetarianism into your life you develop the ability not to identify with the mind's activity when it pursues its dualistic methods.

Let your hands or feet, rather than your mind, lead you somewhere.

Exploring the Mindfield.

The "mindfield" is that area within us that can open to energy or block it. It can fear emotions or trust them. It can force our bodies or it can allow itself to be united with the body. When you experience it as separate from your body, the mind is often fearful. Your mind may see limitations and accept the idea of scarcity. It makes molehill issues mountainous. Your mind may want to be done with the process of changing. But you have to accept that you are—as you will always be, as we all are—a person in process.

Trust your body today.

The mind never offers something generic to us to keep us from the path.

When it comes to spiritual practices, including vegetarianism, we may be plentiful with excuses, "It takes too much time." "It's too hard." "It is the homeless and the hungry who need our attention." "It's not worth it." The mind is so creative! It can tailor our excuses to our own life situations. The mind always speaks to us in all our fragile humanity, appealing to our own individual needs.

Light a candle and make an intention for the day.

Seeing vegetarian cooking as meditation brings consciousness to food preparation.

When we bring consciousness to food preparation, that energy and focus informs us when we eat the food. The work we did to prepare and the thoughts we brought to working with the food are present as we eat. We draw on this energy, making further connections with ourselves.

When you can, work directly with a local farmer, a local gardener, a local orchard grower, or a local tofu producer to obtain your food.

How not to characterize the mind.

In describing the mind's ceaseless restlessness, Buddhist tradition calls this resistance to settling down the "monkey mind." It is mental activity that keeps our minds so busy we are unable to deepen to our hearts. I understand why it's called "monkey mind": Monkeys do seem to be always moving— from tree limb to tree limb, hopping down onto the forest floor, and then swinging back up, chattering.

This incessant movement seems to be enacted by our minds, too. But it is a deceptive label. As far as we know at this time, it is our *humanness*, the way *our* minds work, that creates the experience of duality, the restless chattering, and labels us different from other animals. In attempting to objectify the functioning of the mind, we may actually objectify other animals.

Remind yourself to slow down when you find yourself or your mind racing ahead. Dwell in the moment.

We are never asked to make two next steps at one time;
we are only asked to make the next step.

Failing to keep a promise often occurs because we're
trying to take more than the next step. If you find yourself
unable to keep your promises, you may need to keep one that's
very easy. In making a small promise and then keeping it, your
mind encounters your best kind of energy, and may be able to
move with it.

**Are there any vegetable foods or herbs you might
grow for yourself this year?**

Cultivate flexible thinking.

Flexible thinking is the opposite of all-or-nothing thinking. You may not have taken your next step some time in the past, but that doesn't mean you are never meant to take that next step or that you are unable to take that step. You can think, "I tried it that way once. It didn't work. But maybe that was because that was not the right way for me. I can try it this way."

Plant some herbs—indoors is fine.

Keep promises to yourself by understanding when your "Best" self reveals itself.

For me, my "Best" self appears in the early morning. I try to trust my early-morning self and stay aligned with her during the rest of the day. This doesn't mean that the anxious self, hectoring me about what I did and did not do, isn't there. What it means is that also present is my best self, who draws upon a sense of abundant love and is able to direct me in a very practical way to experience and share this abundance.

If I can find a way to stay connected to this fresh, alive, newly awake part of myself throughout the day, I'm able to keep taking my next step.

Before you get up, take some time to reflect on what it means to rise up to meet the day.

*"Catch" that best self in thought and find out what it
wants.*

Your best self may appear when you are cooking, or
daydreaming, or walking, or relaxing in a bath; it may be a sort
of daydreaming self. By "catching" the best self in thought you
connect to this energy. Then set an appointment with yourself.
By setting an appointment with yourself, you can bring that
best self into the rest of the day. And by keeping the
appointment with that time, you keep an appointment with
the self that wants to walk the spiritual path.

**Set your alarm thirty minutes earlier tomorrow to
see if you can catch your best self.**

Use your calendar.

When you are starting a practice, put it on your calendar. "Yoga: 7:30–8:45." "Fix vegetarian meal: 5:15–6:00." "Write in journal: 7:00–7:15." "Work with dreams: 6:15-6:45."

This may sound forced, but this planning is a witness to your outer-oriented self. You are giving yourself the love and time as you write the dates in, and then, again, as you follow the calendar. Moreover, if you are like those of us who find it difficult to say no to some invitation or another, you now have a good reason to decline: you have a previous commitment.

Use your calendar. Make an appointment with yourself.

I believe we can change.

I believe we can each transform our lives from lives in which attention is absent to lives of attention. This change is not a quick or overnight conversion, but a real lasting change that can permeate every moment of our lives. Such attentiveness miraculously extends our lives not through some change in the quantity of our living, but in the quality of that living.

Thank a friend who believes in you.

During a decade of activism for fair housing practices, I discovered that courage is not so much an act as a commitment to a process.

My experience trying to get low-income housing built in a community was a very difficult time: Disempowering one day, empowering the next, a seesaw of advances and losses. I can be grateful now for the housing battle because it taught a basic spiritual lesson about being courageous. Courage is not so much an act as a commitment to a process. If someone had said to me then, "Carol, before this is through, you will experience torments and betrayals and losses. Are you ready?" I probably would have said, "No. I cannot endure such suffering." But all I needed then was the courage to take the next step. First I and my fellow activists tried education. When that failed, we pursued litigation. When there was a backlash, we consolidated. Each step became the self-evident one because of the previous step. We did not have a map for our path, but we had conviction.

Remember a time when you were courageous. What did you learn?

*Courage is your ability to encounter whatever happens
as you take your next step.*

Your inner self grows to meet the demands that your next
step requires. This is the courage to be: To know that your
inner self meets you on this path. You only have to have the
courage to take the next step.

**Check in: Did you make an appointment with
yourself in your calendar? If so, did you keep it? If
not, are you ready now to commit to a next step?**

Creating something new in the kitchen affirms your cooking, the food, your process, and your creativity.

Creating something new in the kitchen mirrors what is happening inside you. You are creating something new within as well.

Make a vegetarian meal for someone you love.

Your negative assumptions can keep you from taking your next step.

Negative thoughts often become a way of life. "This can't work." "That can't be done." "It is too hard." Negative thoughts and reactions need not dominate our thinking. We are in the process of transformation. These thoughts need transformation, too.

Don't minimize your own abilities, or your own worth, or your own experiences, or your need, unspoken perhaps, to feel connections! Tell yourself, "This *can* work!" "This *can* be done." "If it is my next step, it can't be too hard."

Identify two thoughts you have had that tell you you can't move forward. Convert them into positive statements.

Affirmations help you grow.

The mind does not constantly have to draw upon past experiences and messages that are no longer helpful. Instead, developing affirmations gives your mind new information. Cultivate the art of affirming the spiritual practices that attract your energy. You can do this!

Identify what you wish to bring into your life: Veganism? Daily meditation? Journaling? Activism on behalf of animals? Create an affirmation, "I, [your name] enjoy [veganism/ meditation/journaling, activism, or something else you desire to bring into your life] each day." Repeat it. Write it down. See yourself doing it.

In affirming yourself, accept imperfection.

Tell yourself, "I cannot do this perfectly. If I wait to do this perfectly I may never do it. But I can do something now. I don't have to postpone. I can do this learning as I go. I can accept that I am not further than I am, but I can affirm I am further than yesterday." Accept the confusing imperfection of only taking just one step forward.

Close your eyes, relax, and repeat the affirmation you created yesterday. See yourself practicing your practice as you repeat it several times.

Let the smells of vegetarian cooking invite you home.

Smells penetrate the brain, circumventing the conscious process. Fill your house with the welcoming smells of nourishing food. Let vegetarian cooking invite you home.

Put a mixture of a cinammon stick, some cloves and an orange in two or three cups of water. Bring to a boil and let simmer. Enjoy the smells. Or use apple juice and drink the warmed and spiced juice.

Stay focused on your path.

There will be others who will say, "What's the use of this?" Don't let their critical attitudes influence you. You've got your own critical attitudes inside. Trust me: Working with your own critical self is much more fruitful than succumbing to the negative thoughts of people who aren't taking their own next steps.

You can say, "I know this may not be understandable to you. But I need to be doing this right now. And I would appreciate your support." Sometimes people, especially family and friends, want to keep you locked in the past. That is where they want to stay, too. In taking your next step, you help yourself and others understand what it means to live in the present moment.

Collect two sayings that speak to your heart.

Allow food to express itself in your cooking.

Attentiveness to "peachness," or "orangeness," or "zucchininess." It is a multi-sensuous approach—the peach speaks to you through sight, smell, touch, and perhaps imagination. In experiencing its "peachness," you also experience your relationship to it. "Peachness" teaches you something about yourself.

Go shopping and see what vegetables or fruits speak to you. What vegetables look fresh? What fruit asserts itself? What do they invite you to prepare?

Experiencing the flow of cooking, I cease to be a cook cooking.

I become the process. I feel the peach, or the orange, or the tofu lead me toward the way to prepare it. The food is unfolding something new through me.

After cooking a meal, ask yourself, "What is new about me?" Trust that there is an answer.

If spirituality involves trusting the process, spiritual
practice requires touching the process.

Touching the process means you make a commitment to
practice, and by the very act of keeping that commitment you
begin to experience transformation. In the act of practicing,
whether it be yoga, meditation, keeping a journal, or
vegetarianism, the practice itself begins to work within you.
The process of keeping a commitment will touch you in many
wonderful and unexpected ways.

Make a vegetable bouquet to celebrate
abundance: use flowers or green leaves,
chopsticks, multicolored peppers, tomatoes,
mushrooms, and zucchini. Stick the vegetables on
to the ends of the chopsticks and arrange them
into a bouquet.

Touching the process is the practicing of the practice.

Spiritual practice requires that we involve ourselves. We need not only to place our trust in the process of vegetarianism or spiritual practice, but we need to touch this process and let it touch us. We need to allow ourselves to become immersed. When we don't trust the process, it may be because we're not touching it.

Prepare a meal using the vegetables from yesterday's vegetable bouquet.

> *We cannot be spectators to our own spiritual growth. We*
> *have to touch the process.*

How do you touch the process? Practice your practice. If it is yoga, you practice; if it is vegetarianism, you choose your food accordingly; if it is keeping a journal, you write. These are body-related practices; they involve us. You touch the process to let the process touch you. It will.

Touch the process. Take time for your body today.

Becoming a vegetarian is touching the process.

When it comes to vegetarianism, touching the process is epitomized by being aware of what we are literally taking into our bodies as food. Vegetarians do this by bringing their vegetarian awareness to each activity, again and again. It is a process. The process involves examining the same issues that are embedded within spiritual quests: Who am I? How do I constitute my self? Will I allow vegetarian awareness to inform my life or not? What is desire for wholeness and what is a craving for gratification? Am I isolated from others or do I sense connection? The root of the process is the focusing of energy so vegetarians can make a promise and keep it.

Add a new plant protein source to your diet today.

*Touching the process is how you engage your spiritual
path.*

When we touch the process, we bring to our conscious
mind our previously unexamined contact with the world.
Usually, this awareness manifests itself in those aspects of our
life most in need of healing and repairing. In touching the
process, we let the process become a part of us. We interact
with it, first as an external goal, than as an enacted goal, an
inner reality.

**Notice something that is blossoming today. Is it
you?**

The inner art is faith in the process, staying with the process, and allowing the process to work.

The inner art is a series of next steps linked together into a habit of practice.

Go for a walk today and watch your steps closely. What might your spiritual or vegetarian next step be?

Through "journaling" I have learned how to be honest with myself.

Among other things, vegetarianism requires such honesty.

Check in: Are you journaling? If so, reread your past entries and thank yourself for coming to the page. If not, take ten minutes and write a letter to yourself about what you are feeling today.

Mixing It Up.

We can mix with an electric mixer, fast, mechanical.

Or we can mix with a hand beater.

Or mix with a pastry blender.

Or mix with a wooden spoon.

Mixing it up brings air into the ingredients. If we use baking soda, baking powder, or a sourdough culture in our cooking, we beat them into the mixture knowing they are creating air pockets within the ingredients. The air space causes baked goods to rise, giving them lightness.

Just so, a spiritual practice brings space within us, causing us to rise and making us light.

Learn to bake something today—enjoy the process of expansion.

Does coming together feel like you are breaking apart?

One of my favorite implements is the pastry blender. With it, I mix Succanat™, spelt flour, and vegan margarine together for scones. The separate ingredients are brought together through the tines and a new mixture appears, crumbly but still holding together, too. Most foods become crumbly when they are being broken apart. For scones, being crumbly is a part of their movement toward coming together as a baked good.

In order for us to come together in a new way we need to break down the ingredients and mix them up. We may be confused by this process. We may not understand how breaking apart is an aspect of coming together. But through a spiritual practice we can isolate an aspect of ourselves, to enable our process of growth.

Sit down and tell yourself that for fifteen minutes you will draw or doodle. Discover as you do how you are feeling.

Like focusing on breathing, focusing on cooking creates its own consciousness shift.

Mixing is a rhythmic action. When we mix by hand we allow the rhythms of our actions to act upon ourselves, too. The motions in themselves are calming. Simply by focusing on stirring the muffins and cutting the zucchini, the rhythm, movement, focus, and smells bring about a change, a pause, a deepening. Our wordless self is exploring the relationships. This shift can happen in just an instant when you switch your concentration from the mind's thoughts to the look of the tomato as you cut it.

Thanks to the mixing motion or the chopping motion or the stirring motion, the mind relaxes slightly, and then suddenly lets go! Cooking pulls you deeper.

Identify seven basic vegetarian evening meals you could rely on throughout a month.

The practice of being a vegetarian, like the practices of journaling, yoga, and meditation, transforms us.

Simply by keeping the commitment to the practices we reveal ourselves to ourselves and honor our spiritual self. We bring that self into the conscious actions of our lives, and this enlarges us. The practice itself nurtures us at the level that our conscious mind may not recognize.

Get up early and listen for the first sounds of birds in the morning. What are their songs like at daybreak?

Keeping a journal can help you hear yourself thinking.

Writing in your journal first thing in the morning, you may hear yourself *feeling*.

Ask yourself, "To what have I committed myself in my life so far?" Answer in a journal or in a letter to yourself. Listen to yourself thinking and feeling.

*The process of becoming a vegetarian introduces us to
the self we didn't necessarily know we were.*

When you become a vegetarian you encounter both love
and torments. You love yourself for following your heart; you
feel tormented because you are following your heart. The
torments arise as you learn more about yourself: How much
you are attached to foods you know aren't good for you, or
how hard it is to give up foods that are the result of so much
suffering. You discover how trivial your food needs are and get
embarrassed by how resentful you feel when you're "cheated"
out of the food you want. "So I really am that needy when it
comes to food!" Or worse, "So I really am that petty!"

If you feel constricted and cheated, connect to the
multiple reasons for being vegetarian, and experience love
cultivating itself in you. Love can fill the place where you feel
constricted and dissolve that feeling.

**Do a little deep sea diving today: Wallow in
emotion, drink deeply from the cup of human
kindness, water a tree in your neighborhood.**

As you practice vegetarianism you touch the process of being a vegetarian.

Becoming a vegetarian will reveal its intrinsic joys. In consciously changing our habits, we allow the process to touch us. We may not feel that the practice is having any effect, but we should rest assured that it is at work beneath the level of consciousness. It is registering inside of us and it will manifest itself. That is why we trust the process. We understand we are being touched.

Be firm today: Feel good, be touched, affirm someone else.

Attention is a gift of consciousness.

Practicing being attentive is different from other sets of practices. Attention is required throughout the day. It is a gift of consciousness to be able to approach a table filled with food, and discriminate. Is there harm here? What foods can I embrace and not participate in that harm? This is vegetarian consciousness. Many people fear this gift. They block attention because changing one's diet seems too hard. They don't know that refusing a gift is hard, too.

Write five things you want to have in your life and bury them in a seeded pot. Watch them grow.

The process of focusing energy so we can make a promise and then keep it feels hard because we're not used to bringing this amount of attention to something like eating.

The solution is to love the part of you that is growing in attentiveness and love the part that doesn't want to be attentive, that finds focusing hard. But don't allow "hardness" to keep you from your path.

Get some clay and play with it. Experience what it means to reshape something firm or "hard."

Attention leads to intention.

Once we have fostered attention, we have to use our intention—we have to stick our big toes in. But what if we don't want to stick our toes into the water; what if we don't want to climb onto a raft? First, allow awareness to alert you to what you are responding to and feeling. What are you noticing—needs or demands? Intention does not mean stoicism; we're not talking about the imposition of limitations or denial. This is not control. Attention means we can suspend attachment. Attachment may prevent the flow of energy. With attention, we allow the flow to be connected to consciousness.

Celebrate May Day by taking flowers or a plant to a shut-in or someone who is ill, or leaving a surprise flower basket by someone's front door. Allow intention to flower.

Intention enables detachment.

Detachment means not being product-oriented. At times, it may not feel like detachment—we feel desire for a food and yet we know we don't really want to consume it. But when we've cultivated detachment, we know that messages from the mind about the senses do not need to be identified with. If we experience craving for something, we don't confuse that craving with ourselves. We don't have to identify with the desire; we don't have to think that this is a defining aspect of ourselves. This is detachment. We are able to separate our needs from our mind. We watch our needs arise and we watch them fall away.

I want to stress that I'm not saying we force ourselves to go hungry. Quite the opposite: We don't force anything! We care for ourselves.

Write five things you don't want to have in your life and burn them. Throw the ashes into the wind.

By suspending our need for attachment, we create the space for detachment.

We can then act intentionally toward an item of food. Not needing to "have" it, we don't eat it. We are not imprisoned within the mind's interpretations of a need. Suddenly, we discover the process of being attentive has led us through the water!

Take a walk near water, if possible. If not, take a walk near water in your mind.

Cooking in the Present Moment.

When you are cooking, don't listen to the news on radio or TV. The news you are waiting for is coming from within. Cooking is complete within itself. Don't answer the phone. It will interrupt the flow. But, if there are children around, welcome them into the process. Enjoy the present moment of creating. It is a gift.

While cooking mindfully, experiment with cooking a sea vegetable today.

Cooking changes our consciousness about time.

Time is measured by the rhythm of food preparation and the awakened senses we bring to cooking. Eventually we don't need a timer. We know that tofu is done frying by its golden look in the pan. We know the muffins are baked by their smell, bread by its sound. We poke the roast vegetables to check their firmness. We bring this way of measuring time into other aspects of our lives. We know from within when it is time to move on, to let go, to marinate our souls in supportive environment.

If you bake, bake something special. If not, walk into a bakery and smell its wonderful smells.

Every spiritual quest involves temptation.

Stories of the temptation of Jesus Christ or the Buddha make temptation sound very dramatic and the subsequent responses to those temptations revelatory. But in today's world the temptations may manifest themselves in seemingly undramatic ways—decisions about lunch and then again about dinner. The voice is not of some disembodied or powerful agent of attachment, it's the voice of your best friend or your co-worker. "Come on, one fish fry won't matter." But it is still "temptation" and it helps to understand that temptation is always a part of a spiritual quest.

Take a curious, receptive nonvegetarian friend out to a vegetarian restaurant.

Like many spiritual practitioners, vegetarians discipline
their mind.

The mind knows our weaknesses and appeals directly to them since it, more than the stomach, is cued to the stimuli of the outside world. The mind doesn't want to lose control. It wants to continue its own self-absorbed dialogue. The mind wants to stay hooked to the outside world and it does so by exploiting whatever is your central weakness. This is one way the conditioned mind battles for control. You can take comfort that your mind knows you so well.

Share an inspirational thought with a friend.

The same overactive mind that distracts a meditator and tries to carry on its own dialogue tries to distract the vegetarian.

A meditator doesn't cling to a thought that's entered her mind; she acknowledges it as a thought and returns to focusing on her breath. A vegetarian does the same. Both recognize that even though the conditioned mind's experience of reality is limited, this mind wants to maintain control. The temptation is to let it. Both the meditator and the vegetarian do not succumb to the temptation that distracts them from their meditative practice. They know that reality is larger than that thought in the case of meditation, or that piece of "whatever," in the case of vegetarianism. The problem for many people is that the piece of "whatever" may appear a lot more substantial than the thought distracting the meditator. But they are the same temptation, and they both require a mind that knows how to bring attentiveness to the living of one's life.

Sit and listen quietly to all the familiar sounds of your house that you are not usually aware of.

Detachment changes consciousness.

Through detachment, some "foods" simply cease to be seen as food. One's consciousness can experience meat and dairy and eggs as "not food." There is then no process of attraction and examination of this attraction when they are present. There is no beckoning. There may be a sadness for the world because it is still using animals as food sources, but the detachment announces the integration of consciousness and action. It announces transformation. You have successfully taken a next step!

Allow yourself to feel sadness for the world because it is still using animals as food sources. Create a grieving ritual that acknowledges that this sadness is okay. Find a way to release the sadness.

Vegetarianism is a blessing.

In any day, I may move through turmoil and stress, sadness and conflict, whether internal or external, but when I eat my vegetarian meal, I am brought into the present. Wherever I go, I know that vegetarian food will bid me welcome—even if I carry it in my backpack as insurance. When I make mistakes and reproach myself for some failure, my vegetarianism affirms me. When I have self-doubts, false starts, and misdirected energy, vegetarianism grounds me. Vegetarianism is a blessing.

List five ways vegetarianism has enhanced your life or could enhance your life.

Mixing ingredients together is the outer manifestation
of an internal mixing together.

Vegetarian cooking is playful! Look at dumplings—a doughy concoction that cooks in broth. When you add baking soda to a mixture that contains vinegar in it (this is a famous old recipe for a delicious cake), wow! What a bubbling, frothing, growing reaction! This playfulness is in and of itself healing because it derails the left brain's serious train of thought. Indeed, it might be the integration of left and right brain in cooking that gives us so much pleasure.

Take time to be playful today.

> *Vegetarianism teaches us how a spiritual practice becomes "spontaneous."*

When a practice is spontaneous, it is present to us. But for many it seems that in becoming a vegetarian nothing feels spontaneous. Everything has to be planned, anticipated, interrogated. Each time we act consciously on behalf of our vegetarianism, the more that we tip our vegetarianism back towards spontaneity. The practice of being a vegetarian itself pulls us forward. We trust that even in the absence of the spontaneous, we are creating the inner conditions for spontaneity.

Start a vegetarian survival bag for trips, visits, and other times when your need for vegetarian food might not be met.

In the first stage of accessing our inner art, our spiritual practice may be something that feels imposed.

Even when it arises from our own best desires, in the beginning a spiritual practice imposes on our old habits. During this first stage, spiritual practice requires deliberateness. We consciously plan our day to incorporate vegetarianism and perhaps other spiritual practices. In becoming vegetarians, what once was spontaneous—eating— becomes ritualized. We take the time to plan a meal or a restaurant trip to insure that it has the plant-based food we need. And we understand that this is only one aspect of a vegetarian path.

Look at the vegetables at a natural foods store. What vegetables have you never eaten? Make a promise to try one.

In the second stage of accessing our inner art, we know our vegetarianism or another spiritual practice has begun to become a habit when its absence creates a feeling of incompleteness.

Did we miss meditation or yoga today, or not have a vegetarian meal? We are aware of absence. That is good! Paradoxically, absence announces what our consciousness is making present: Our practice is evolving into a spontaneous action.

Give thanks today for having a home, clothes, a job, family, a lover/spouse/child, money, friends, talent, prospects, life, and hope. Give thought to those—human and non-human—who don't, and imagine what it would be like not to have these things.

In the third stage, our spiritual practice has become a spontaneous action, without which we feel incomplete.

In this stage, we don't have to debate with ourselves or negotiate about our practice. It's a part of our lives. As much as sleeping, or eating, it is a part of our day. When it has become a need, we shape our lives to ensure it's not absent. It has becomes an expression of our inner self.

Try praying.

The nature of an inner art is revealed as both ritual and spontaneity together.

Here is an example: Mr. Rogers enters through the door. He removes his jacket and puts on his zippered cardigan. Then he sits down, methodically removes his shoes, and puts on a pair of navy-blue sneakers. Every time his show begins, Mr. Rogers changes his jacket, removes his shoes. One day, Mr. Rogers visited Koko, a gorilla who uses American Sign Language and who had watched *Mr. Rogers' Neighborhood*. First, Koko enfolded him in her arms in a big hug. Then Koko took Mr. Rogers's sneakers off. Mr. Roger's and Koko's rituals enabled this spontaneous moment to occur. This is the inner art.

Think about your day and be grateful for the things that happened. Have you experienced ritual and spontaneity together?

As we develop the habit of vegetarianism what has been
willed becomes so necessary to who we are that it has the
fresh feeling of both necessity and spontaneity.

Through practice we return again and again to the same
action—yet a spiritual practice, paradoxically, creates a habit
that presumes and acknowledges impermanence. Spiritual
practice links itself to the positive nature of constant change.
And we rejoice in this nature. That is our hug from the
universe.

Touch a part of your body and really feel around.
What does touching yourself in that part make
you feel?

We are always changing!

The maxim that "one cannot cross the same river twice" refers not only to the changing river, whose waters are constantly flowing forward. We are changing, too.

From the moment we place our big toe in it, we are different. Crossing the river changes us. By touching the process of cultivating a spiritual practice, we have made a habit of change.

Be thankful for someone who has helped you cross the river. If you can, let them know of your thankfulness.

Food is one of the ways we grasp at the mirage of permanence.

As Krishnamurti observes, we are "afraid of the known coming to an end." Like nonspiritually oriented individuals, spiritual practitioners may cling to the past. Some grasp onto the past through grasping to old food habits, "I have always eaten it this way!" We may look to food to find a guarantee or confirmation of permanence. We forget the lesson of the moving waters.

Watch flowers die. What does it mean to wilt? Reflect on how energy is transferred from living to dying and then to new life.

Part of the human dilemma is that we defend ourselves against impermanence.

Impermanence afflicts us. We are afraid of our own deaths. We try to cling to the permanent, but we cannot actually grasp it, because nothing is permanent except impermanence. The challenge is to become freed by this insight, rather than grasp at the mirage of permanence. If only we could accept that we and the people we love most will die, then we could be free from fear and embrace living in the present moment. We would be alive to the present moment because that is all we have.

Imagine what it would be like to have a loved one taken from you.

*Some people may fear becoming vegetarians because
they are clinging to permanence.*

People who are fearful of becoming vegetarians hold on to
old habits as though that will make life more permanent. Here
we discover a relationship between our fear of our own death
and our willingness to require the deaths of so many billions
of animals each year. This resistance to dealing with our own
mortality may be that which allows us to take the deaths of
animals so lightly. We deaden ourselves to death. We deny our
fear, and thus deny feeling.

**Take a moment to grieve over someone you know
who is dead and whom you haven't thought about
in a while. What gifts did they give you? Think of
something you wished you had said, and say it
aloud to yourself.**

*Those who are fearful of change may be eating that fear
instead.*

Animals suffer in their living and their dying. Chefs
recognize this when they choose fishes according to how they
died. Fishes are stressed by being caught. The more stressed the
fishes are, the more lactic acid they have in their flesh. The
animals' fear is in their lactic acid. When animals pump
adrenaline and endorphins before they are killed, these enter
their muscles. Those who are fearful of change may be eating
that fear instead.

**Has there been a moment in your life when you
were scared to die? If there has, try and recall what
your body felt like. If there hasn't, try and imagine
what your body might feel like.**

Vegetarian cooking might be defined as the stringing together of moments of impermanence.

Because of impermanence we cannot hold on to things. Cooking teaches us this. We cooks know what impermanence is. We have touched it. What was grown and then made is eaten and vanishes. Yet it is transformed into life. Because of our awareness of this constant change, we can experience moments of connections, free of illusions.

List possible vegetarian breakfasts.

Impermanence gives us something; it doesn't take something away.

We embrace impermanence by following the seasons. Many vegetarian recipe books arrange their recipes according to seasons. Winter recipes feature vegetable stews and chilies. Summer recipes often require less cooking—salads, cold soups. By basing our foods on the seasons, we are more likely to have a varied diet than nonvegetarians; and in that variety we have mirrored before us the poetry of growth, fruition, and harvest. Yesterday the first asparagus of spring were in; now they are gone.

By following the seasons, we harmonize ourselves with our environment. We are in tune with a rhythm of life and we are blessed by it.

Reach out to a child today—or reach in to the child in yourself.

Sourdough is an ingredient and a process.

From flour and water comes a mixture that transforms other things. If the conditions are right, you can leave the flour and water outside, and beat it several times a day, and those invisible yet vitally important parts of sourdough—lactobacilli and wild yeast—will settle into your mixture. By the third day, your mixture is a bubbling, frothing culture. If you stick your hand into the bubbling mixture of flour, water, wild yeasts, and lactobacilli, you can burst the bubbles. It's that alive!

This is how we add a spiritual practice to our life: we take the basic materials of our lives, and we take the time to let them be. We isolate them and let them find new relationships. We let air work on our unrisen selves, on breathing, or on our body's movements.

Create order—in your house, or your desk—so your energy can flow unimpeded.

Our spirits, once awakened, want to be fed.

Once a sourdough culture exists, it must be fed or refrigerated. Our spirits, once awakened, want to be fed, too. We feed our spirits by bringing ourselves to the yoga mat, or to the meditation cushion, or to the kitchen, or to our journal.

Check in: Have you made an appointment with yourself? If so, did you act on your calendar's notation? If not, make one today.

Balance in life is like balance in sourdough bread.

When it looks as though nothing is happening to sourdough bread dough during its rest time in the refrigerator, something is: It is becoming infused with taste. The lactobacilli are having time to work. The wild yeast is like the part of us that is active. But if we let the wild yeast in us overwhelm the lactobacilli, we won't have balance, nor will our bread be tasty. We need the rest time, too.

Identify three ways to waste time positively. Try to do one of them.

Like sourdough cultures, we are each unique.

Each sourdough culture is unique. Some cultures are fast-acting, and the bread rises in a couple of hours. Others work at a much slower pace. We have to know our cultures to produce good bread.

We have to know ourselves. With a sourdough culture, you can make light, tasty pancakes in seconds. All you have to do is add a little baking soda to your culture and drop it onto a warm griddle.

We can make the way for change, five minutes at a time.

Go outside and look at the sky for five minutes

It is what is inside that counts.

With a sourdough culture, you influence the course of bread baking. By adding half a cup or one cup of culture—that is all!—to a bread recipe, we can dispense with domestic yeast. The sourdough infuses the dough, changing the course of its growth. In the same way, our spiritual practices do not require that we devote all our time to them. But by our commitment, of ten minutes or an hour, or two, we influence the course of our waking and our sleeping.

When you wake up, call to mind all of the things you are thankful for. They can be mundane. Throughout the day, remind yourself of these aspects of your life that you are thankful for.

We always have to reserve that cup.

With a sourdough culture, you can always have more. Recipe books always remind you before you start cooking with sourdough to reserve a cup. By reserving a cup, you have the building blocks for the next recipe.

Likewise, when we go out and mix it up in the world, we must beware of depleting ourselves so thoroughly that there's nothing left. We always have to reserve that cup.

Blow dandelion seeds into the wind. Try and follow one until it falls to the ground.

Sourdough baking teaches me that a cyclical movement of rising and falling is a part of life.

We bring our entire body to kneading the dough. We feel the strength of our arms, the legs grounding us. How we are balanced influences the energy we bring to kneading. All of me kneads the dough. I look at my sourdough bread dough as it follows the process before baking and I see this: It rises, it falls. The fall is part of the rising. We rise, we fall, we cycle through life.

Look at the shadows cast by the sun as it moves through the day. Think about the arc of the day and the arc of your day. Do you allow time for both rising *and* falling?

Touch the process!

We know where the dough is in the process of becoming bread by touching it. Poke it during the rising stage; if it doesn't bounce back, it is done rising. Tap it on the bottom when you think it should be done baking, and if you hear a hollow thud you are right, it is.

It took discipline to learn about sourdough. I had to introduce something new into my repertoire. But, if I so choose, I can write until 7:15 a.m. and know that sourdough pancakes will be ready at 7:30. Now I can make the most delectable vegan cakes—with sourdough. Now I can give away sourdough culture so that others can make pancakes or sweets.

Now I teach others. I am a part of the process.

Take a walk and offer thanks for what you encounter on your path.

By working with our dreams, we treat them as living aspects of our personality.

By working with dreams, we honor the part of us that expresses itself through dreams. This part of us wants to be known, too. Dreams offer us wholeness. In the face of the healing nature of dreams, why should we settle for only fractions of a life?

Have you dreamt about a friend or family member? Give her or him a call.

To step into the flow of cooking, meet the world at your skin.

Sometimes, when I'm aware of energy pulsating through me, my cells feel particularly alive. I know this because I am aware of my skin. My skin is the threshold between inner and outer. Literally, when I am writing, my energy is meeting the world at my fingertips because this is the place where I hold my pen or type into the keyboard. I feel this aliveness at times when I am writing.

But I also feel it when I'm cooking: When my fingers peel the skin off a garlic clove, or slip the skin off a roasted red pepper, or retain the smell of fresh basil on their tips after making pesto. I feel myself being connected to creation and I step into the flow of cooking.

Rub your hands together vigorously for several seconds and then touch your hands to different parts of your body. What do you feel?

I trust there is a healing process going on in my unconscious.

One day, as I was making a mushroom cobbler, I became aware of not feeling grounded. My energy was darting all over the place. Then I looked at the onions, which had been simmering at very low heat for about an hour, allowing them to get soft and caramelized. There was nothing for me to do. I had to allow them this process.

The same is true when I'm meditating. I must also let be. There is nothing I must do. Just as something is happening with that onion as it cooks, something is happening with me, too. I can't see it happening, but I know it happens—I'm being made tender.

Take the time and really listen to someone carefully—perhaps yourself.

Prepare to step into the process of vegetarian cooking.

Plan your meals when you're relaxed and refreshed. If you know your evening energy is rushed, unthinking, and tired, don't leave it until the evening to decide what supper will be. Instead, select the recipe earlier in the day or before you go to bed the night before. Create the conditions for cooking. Your intentional placement of attention earlier becomes an invitation for your energy. That earlier step has prepared the way for this next step. Then, when the time comes, you can step into the process of cooking you began earlier.

Identify five comfort foods and make sure you have them available.

Spiritual practices help us interpret the world in a more symbolic manner.

Leaning how to think symbolically is important because our right and left brains take in information in very different ways. The conscious mind works through being ceaselessly verbal. It manages information through a hum of words and word associations that the conscious mind structures. On the other hand, the unconscious mind is nonverbal. When the conscious and unconscious minds encounter symbols and metaphors, both halves work together.

Write down a dream and give it a title.

Literal thinking is a beginning, not an end.

Becoming a vegetarian often involves thinking very literally. For instance, meat is not "meat"; it is muscle from a corpse. Milk involves the enslavement of cows and the robbing of nourishment from their own calves. Eggs are reproductive secretions. While literal thinking is important in perceiving the world, especially when the issue is animal exploitation, literal thinking can also trip up all of us—including vegetarians. It can prevent us from thinking symbolically, from being playful, from following our spiritual path. Not every aspect of life should be taken only literally.

How have you been overly literal in your thinking? During your day, playfully describe things around you using metaphors and similes.

Your Own "Aha!"

If you hear on the radio that two whales are stranded in some ice, you may create a picture in your mind of the whales swimming around, trapped. You might also think about what this means, and why these two particular whales are caught. The right and left brain are each processing this information in their own way. The conscious mind has questions, the unconscious mind, associations. When encountering a symbol or metaphor, the conscious and the unconscious respond to it along different tracks, until suddenly—and often with a feeling of "aha!"—they come together and we "know" something. We experience a connection and something opens up that wasn't there before.

Visit a pond, a lake, a stream, or an ocean near you and enjoy seeing fishes in their natural setting. What is swimming around within?

The Benefits of Thinking Symbolically.

Symbols transform conscious awareness by connecting us to a larger reality. When we think symbolically we can detach from the need for a product, from the need to be future oriented, from a solid ego. Instead, we experience the joy of connections in the present time. The "aha!" reorients us.

Write down a dramatic experience that really happened, but write about it as though it was a dream.

philosophy of FREEDOM

Dreams are revelations with a slant.

Dreams are not teaching you something you already know, but something you need to know but have not acknowledged. They are the language of the heart. The problem for most of us is that we do not speak the heart's language. But, we can learn.

Recall your dream. Is there something from the dream that you could do today or incorporate into your life?

Dreams want to be known.

To work with dreams we need to remember them. This is much simpler than people think, because dreams want to be remembered. When the dreaming self insists on being remembered, it comes to us as a nightmare. Dreams want to be known, because they come in the service of wholeness.

Write a summary of a dream in which something violent happened, using as many descriptive words as possible. What was happening to you? What was threatening in your dream? What aspect of your life does it represent?

The process of making friends with your dreams is a process of bringing them into your waking life.

If, in the morning, you allow your dreams to be remembered, they can tell you something about what you have experienced. If, throughout the day, you allow your dreams to speak to you, you will remember more of them. They will feel the energy that connects to the symbolic, experiential, and unconscious aspects of yourself. If, before you go to sleep, you allow yourself to think about being a dreamer and a dream rememberer, your dreams will honor this energy.

Morning, afternoon, evening, nighttime—your dreaming self can be a part of your life.

Look at two recent dreams together. What is their relationship to each other and to your present life?

Dreams speak to us through symbolic language.

Symbolic language may not be a language we understand well. But one interesting way to become open to the dream's language is by living a part of your waking life as though it were a dream: the car is a metal turtle; a walk through a forest of young, thin trees takes you through "snake city;" a tree stump is a troll's rump. By describing your waking life in this way you create more fluidity between the conscious and unconscious parts of yourself, making your dreaming symbols more connected to you.

Think of symbolic ways of describing: this book, the way you are right now, the room you are in, whatever activity you are about to do.

By working with a dream or a dream fragment, you bear witness to your dreaming self that you want to know what you're dreaming.

That act will call forth more dreams. As you write down your dream or dream fragment, tell yourself how important this dream is so that you can defeat any restlessness in the mind that questions why you're bothering. You're giving an answer, "Because it is important."

Write down a dream and see what you feel as you are writing.

Dreams teach us about our fears.

We are the playwrights and the dream is the stage on which we script our fear—whether it is of separation, failure, being in love, or of not being loved. Mistriggered fear, like anxiety, is a distraction from the present moment. Fear keeps us from being present to ourselves. Our dreams show us what our fears are and ask us to be present to ourselves.

See your dream as a photograph or a picture and recall it during your day. What do you learn about yourself?

When you work with dreams, do so in a way that isn't controlling.

Be open to the dream so that its meaning can unfold for you. Do you see it as a photograph? Allow the dream to be a living, glowing thing, given to you, waiting to be interacted with, and speaking to you of your wholeness.

You can work with the dream symbols directly. Start a dialogue with your dream symbol. "Who are you?" you can ask the symbol. "Why are you here now? What do you want? What do you mean?" Allow time for the dream symbol to answer.

Dreams often signal the direction our lives should be flowing.

Although it is difficult, at times, to heed them, dreams come to give us wholeness. Your dreaming self understands this. The challenge is to help our conscious self to experience this.

Have you ever dreamt about being in a car? Are you the driver or a passenger? Is it going slowly or quickly? Backward or forward? Is this car ride a possible metaphor for your life at the moment?

Slow down.

When we slow down, we allow ourselves time to register impressions. We can receive the world, including the world on our plate. Cultivate the art of slowing down when you eat. The most effective way you can do this is by making a commitment to yourself that you will only eat sitting down. Receive the miracle of the harvest each time you eat: sit down and eat.

Take your time today; slow down. Try writing with your nondominant hand. This automatically slows you down. Try walking at a slower pace, talking at a slower pace, eating at a slower pace.

Receive the miracle of the harvest each time you eat.

Taking the time to cook and eat with awareness of the present moment is multi-sensuous: we see, smell, and feel the food and then we are given a second miracle! We taste it. As we receive the miracle of the harvest, we too become an aspect of this fruition.

Focus on a favorite smell. What does its aroma fill you with?

Cooking Without Attachment.

At the point at which he or she sits down, the cook must be like a meditator, having no expectations. She mustn't live in the past in which she prepared the food or cling to that effort at the table. A cook does not cook to be loved, but to express love. So the cook must let go and trust the process.

Let go of an old wound today; release a hurt from the past and feel the freedom of being here now.

A Cooking Meditation at the Summer Solstice.

Breathing in, I feel a spirit of love and compassion for myself.

Breathing out, I am thankful.

Breathing in, I feel the spirit of the growers, especially organic growers, who have grown this food.

Breathing out, I thank them.

Breathing in, I feel the spirit of the cookbook authors and recipe inventors who have helped me on my path.

Breathing out, I thank them.

Breathing in, I feel the presence of the people whom I will be feeding.

Breathing out, I thank them.

Breathing in, I feel the presence of a person who is starting on this path.

Breathing out, I thank her or him.

Breathing in, I know that everything changes.

Breathing out, I step into the river of change. I cook.

Take your seat. If you feel your back slump, sit on a pillow or a chair. Repeat each couplet several times, feeling yourself becoming more centered. Devote about fifteen minutes to it.

---

*Cooking without attachment means not mixing your
ego needs into the meal.*

What people want is good food in a loving atmosphere,
with no judging or expectations. "Engage in action devoid of
attachment," says the *Bhagavad Gita*. When we approach
cooking as a meditation practice we can do precisely that. Yes,
we cooked food to get to the point of eating it. But we did not
engage in the process of cooking only to get to the point of
eating. That makes all the difference.

**Give thanks for the time during which you
prepare the meal and during which you eat, for
the food, for the companionship, for the present
moment.**

Cooking without attachment makes connections.

When we cook without attachment, our legs become the roots of the tree on which the peach grew—the peach in our hand being made into gingered fruit crisp. Our hands become the branches that touch the entire process of growth, the sun's energy, and the rain. Through cooking, we are constantly making connections. We can make other connections as well. We connect to those who will be eating the food and those who have no food to eat.

Run your hand along a tree trunk. What connections do you experience?

Cleaning up says, "I'll be back."

Alan Davidson, the author of *The Oxford Companion to Food*, recommends seeing "washing up" or "doing the dishes" as "the climax of the whole cycle (gathering, preparation, cooking, eating) and as a piece of ritual.... The purification of the utensils has to be the final, culminating stage of any meal, the stage which in effect sets the scene for the next meal and permits life processes to continue."

By taking the time and thought to clean up, we attest to the time and thought involved in preparing food. We remind ourselves of the joyful opportunity to eat food that hasn't required the suffering and death of other animals. Cleaning up says, "I'll begin again." In cleaning up, we complete the circle.

Remind yourself that "every moment is a moment." Bring awareness to the task of cleaning up, the task of restoration.

The desire to change can at one point feel fresh and galvanizing.

But often we feel the burden of not changing, and the desire to change taunts us. We can become so hard and unforgiving of ourselves! My vision of change is a much more gentle, inviting, and affirming process. Rather than creating a litany of "shoulds," we use the practice of attention to move from present moment to present moment. We can give ourselves the gifts of awakening and deepening through a daily practice of thoughtfully engaging with one idea, one meditative thought, one piece of fruit, one vegetarian meal at a time.

Clean out the vegetable compartment in your refrigerator. Make a soup with what you can and acknowledge that some of your vegetables may need to be composted.

*Vegetarians know how to bring attention to our meals;
we can bring it to other parts of our day as well.*

Vegetarians can consciously apply the process of being a vegetarian, and the rituals associated with it, to other aspects of our lives. Attentiveness moves from meal to moment. It accompanies us in our day. It becomes a practice of living as well as of eating. We know how to cultivate vegetarian consciousness; we can cultivate spiritual consciousness in the same way. Other spiritual practices will then deepen the rhythms and rituals of a vegetarian life. We can look, smell, touch, choose, and be in tune with a rhythm of life.

Look, smell, and touch something. What are your senses teaching you?

Being plentiful with excuses keeps us from beginning again.

In *Long Quiet Highway*, Natalie Goldberg describes how much resistance her mind presented when she was trying to realize her desire to create a writing practice. She discovered that the mind is "plentiful with excuses." Among the ones the mind offered her were, "It's too hot. I'm too tired. My house is messy. My stomach hurts. I had a hard day. I'm lonely. I'm not lonely. I'm too happy, too excited, too broke." We are all plentiful with excuses. What Goldberg knew was that that may all be true: It may be too hot. You may be too tired. Chores may beckon. Your body may resist. Your emotions may feel scattered. Yes, that may all be true; but nevertheless, we can begin again.

Keep it in the positive: Let go of what cannot be changed and focus on what is possible.

Being plentiful with excuses keeps us trapped in the past.

When we are trapped in the past we are unable to realize our own heart's longing. The mind doesn't want this change. It desires something solid, knowable, safe, and secure, in preference to what is slippery, unknowable, unstable, changing. It would rather be aware of feeling hot, feeling uncomfortable, feeling the need to make lists and then follow them, or the need to collapse and not follow them. This is what resistance is.

Try a new vegan recipe today.

> *That consciousness in our life that we fail to integrate is*
> *like dragging a stone downhill.*

Yiddish folklore includes tales about a town of fools. These "wise men of Khelm" act in absurd and inappropriate ways. One of my favorite stories concerns the time the entire town decided to move a huge stone on top of a high hill. They went to the top of the hill and started to drag the stone down. When they were about halfway down the hill, a stranger came upon the scene. "Why are you dragging the stone?" the stranger asked them, laughing. "If you simply push the rock it will go down the hill on its own." The Khelmites thought him very wise and took his advice to heart. So, they pulled the stone back up to the top of the hill, pushed it, and, remarkably, that stone rolled to the bottom of the hill all by itself! The stone we're dragging downhill is that consciousness in our life that we fail to integrate, and so we end up dragging it around with us rather than allowing it to follow its natural course.

Go for a walk and look for interesting rocks and stones as a touchstone to being grounded.

Excuses announce we're dragging something around.

When the old and the comfortable feel more attractive than the new and the challenging, we become stone-draggers, thinking we must drag the stone of resistance everywhere, even downhill. We explain why we don't do something we've desired to do, why we can't change, or why we won't attempt something. This takes a lot of work!

Is there something heavy that you are dragging around within you? Is there something you need to release to gravity's pull?

We each have an astigmatism when looking at ourselves.

Excuses are the way we see when our vision is uncorrected; spiritual practice corrects the astigmatism—we can look inward, be inward, we can bring the inner self out. To those excuses that insulate us, anchoring us to past behaviors, we can say, as we do to our wandering thoughts in meditation, "Oh, hello excuse, I've heard you before. Weren't you just here yesterday?"

Pick a tree you see most days and follow it through the seasons.

Cultural conditioning makes the stone we are dragging much heavier.

Cultural conditioning reinforces tradition, puts its weight on conformity, resists change. Anyone who tries to be a vegetarian knows this. Indeed, one way to encounter one's own cultural conditioning is by becoming a vegetarian. The responses, our own and others', bring the burden of cultural conditioning more fully into the open.

Spiritual practice lightens our load. Spiritual practice brings cultural conditioning to consciousness and allows us to examine whether we wish to continue the actions that we learned so well. Spiritual practice is the tool for discovering one's true self, for bringing ego, mind, and heart together.

Go with a friend to visit an ethnic grocery store. Explore the store's vegetables and the vegetable protein sources.

A law of spiritual nature is that we have our own internal pull.

Being plentiful with excuses about why we haven't changed, about why we are still dragging our stone, is part of the human condition. We refuse to recognize the laws of nature and allow gravity's pull to help us. When we recognize that the mind is doing its thing in generating excuses, we are reminded that there is an alternative to dragging the stone. We can allow that internal pull to work its own magic. We can release the stone.

Have a siesta. What does it mean to let the body rest in the heat of the day?

One's inner life is just as worthy, just as important, as one's outside life.

We may be dragging a stone of unworthiness. When one feels unworthy, at least the stone tells us we have something to do. We have to keep dragging it. This keeps us hooked to the demands of the outer world; all is gravity, there is no levity. The person without a spiritual practice may fear "there is nothing inside." Or, more specifically, "there is nothing worthy inside." But so much exists inside! For vegetarians, releasing the stone may involve learning to trust that one has an inner life, that it is worth getting to know, and then getting to know it, to begin to touch the universe inside.

Celebrate new beginnings with a vegetarian barbecue.

One of the biggest stones we may be dragging is the belief that we must be autonomous, able to make it on our own.

Consequently, we experience ourselves as separate from others. Being separate, and with rigid beliefs that refuse to acknowledge our own neediness, we may be afraid of our neediness. We also become afraid to reveal our neediness to others. This belief in autonomy becomes a two-way trap. It keeps us from drawing on the strengths and love of others. And the individual has to defend herself against her own neediness, his own vulnerability. A sense that you have to be independent, to make it on your own, closes off relationships with yourself and with others.

Go through your old photos and give away some to those people who would enjoy them. Let this action remind you of how you are connected to others.

Excuses reveal what we are afraid to encounter.

When nonvegetarians say that becoming a vegetarian is too hard, I hear them saying, "I am afraid to grow. I am afraid of change. I don't want to focus."

When both vegetarians or nonvegetarians say that they don't have the time or enough energy to change, their issue is scarcity. Time, frankly, is the only thing we do have. These particular excuses announce something deeper: They say, "I do not want to encounter what is inadequate or incomplete about myself."

Remind yourself, "I have the time to practice my practice. This practice is worth it. I am worth this practice."

"Hardness" asks us to inquire into its nature.

What is *too* hard? Anything that requires the training of the mind, the refocusing of attention. It may seem hard to make unconscious food choices conscious and to say no to some foods. What feels hard is the focusing of attention. We do this to turn our mind in a new direction. When attention enables intention, food choices can become freer. Attention can be spontaneous. In the presence of attention, hardness dissolves.

Try making miso soup. All you need is water or broth, a carrot, scallions, cubed tofu, a tablespoon or two of miso, and some soy sauce. Bring the water or broth to a boil, simmer the carrot, add the tofu. Dissolve the miso in a few tablespoons of hot water. Add to the soup, along with the scallions and soy sauce. Enjoy.

Let your mind roll down the hill.

Intentional energy dissolves hardness. It can be the energy of letting go. Sometimes we need simply to see something from a different position. When someone says to me, "It's too hard to change," I want to say, "It's okay. You think you have to push the stone up the hill, but you don't." I want to say, "I believe in you. Let your mind roll down the hill."

Say something nice to someone. Let them know you believe in them.

Look for clarity.

Excuses overwhelm us with a scattering of ideas, regrets, and thoughts. There is no clarity, no focus. Nonvegetarians often think they are offering focused excuses, but most often their discussions are all over the map. Spiritual practices teach us the ability to focus. When we experience an aspect of our lives that is unfocused, we are learning that our spiritual practice has not touched us in this place. More than the content of the excuses, the lack of clarity in the excuses themselves announces the presence of unfocused energy.

Try and do one thing at a time and concentrate on the task. Enjoy the small pleasures of being focused.

With attention, we examine the process of making excuses.

The more excuses we provide, the more blocked energy exists around that issue. As we work with our excuses and examine them, we accept their existence but do not accept their dictates. We become attentive.

In the presence of attention, blocked energy is given the opportunity to tell us why it is blocked. What need did we bury?

Do a little earthwork today: Bury a hatchet, uncover a talent, dig up an old friend.

*The constant pull of gravity on that stone as we drag it
can keep us from being playful.*

Seriousness can be a sign that there is chronic anxiety, that
the mind's excuses have become our way of life. If everything
has to be taken seriously, what is needed is not an argument
with our own or someone else's excuses, but playfulness.

**Play with your (vegetarian) food! Make root
vegetables into block prints by carving something
on their ends and inking them and pressing them
onto paper.**

We come to our senses by cooking with them.

Our lips touch, our tongue tastes, our nose smells, our ears listen, our eyes see, our heart loves. It happens in an instant, when the bread is baked, when the first bubble erupts from the soymilk roux simmering for a comforting soup, when the pesto attains the right balance of basil, miso, garlic, walnuts, and olive oil. Our senses tell us we are alive—this very moment!

Decide what to eat based on your sense of smell. What would you enjoy smelling?

Change means learning to value something enough to incorporate it into our lives.

What we need to do is to rejoice in change. It's so much easier to follow gravity's pull than to use exertion to push away from it. That is what is really hard!

Take a moment during the day to plant your feet firmly on the ground. Feel what it is like to be grounded.

Rainer Maria Rilke's advice in Letters to a Young Poet
is advice to anyone on a spiritual path.

If the young poet, after searching himself, discovers that
above all he must write, then the next step, writes Rilke, is to
"Build your life according to this necessity; your life even into
its most indifferent and slightest hour must be a sign of this
urge and a testimony to it." Rilke is talking about how to
organize one's life so that, even in its dailiness and
ordinariness, it points toward something meaningful.

**Write an author whose writings have touched you
and thank them.**

An invisible thread exists in our life that unites its disparate parts.

We tend to think change happens on a grand scale, but if we start by changing the "least" in our lives, we create a movement that will emanate throughout the day. The least important must point to the most important. The things we do that we value or enjoy the least, those aspects of our lives that represent the lack of attraction or interest—ten minutes here and ten minutes there—this is where change has to begin. All these throw-away moments that might keep us inattentive, we instead start to value. Grab those ten minutes out of a day to meditate, practice yoga, study a recipe book, or prepare tofu steaks. All these moments that we make intentional become a part of the thread of our lives.

Take a moment during the day to imagine a piece of string being pulled upward through the top of your head. Feel what it is like to stand tall. Can you imagine the string lifting your heels up?

Caring for the least does not prevent caring for anyone else.

If we, thinking hierarchically, view animals as the least, what we do to them must point (again thinking hierarchically) to the most, the cherishing of human life. In fact, reorganizing our relationship to the least in our lives liberates us from the hierarchical creation of "leasts." What if the least is really the most? It is in the least, the ordinary, the daily that we reveal and experience our spirituality. As we develop the ability to thread concern of the "least" throughout our day, we discover that such compassionate concern touches our relationships with others, too. Rather than restricting our ability to love, caring for the "least" expands our capacity to love.

Enjoy the details of life: Can you see the difference between a cricket and a grasshopper?

Excuses say, "I have not valued this."

The fact, however, that we make excuses at all announces that we feel some sort of duty to the least. If we did not feel this duty, we wouldn't feel the need to explain our lack of attention. We are in essence saying, "I have not valued this sufficiently to act, and yet I value it sufficiently to have it in my consciousness." Our choice is to excuse our lack of action, or to integrate consciousness and action. Excuses say, "I have not valued this," but they also reveal, "I would like to learn how to...if I could change."

Check in: Did you take your next step? If so, what is your next one now? If not, what do your excuses teach you?

*Because of our conditioned mind, we tend to live lives
in reverse: The most becomes the least.*

The person who wishes to write but doesn't know how to
accept that desire may design her or his life denying that
desire. The commitment these people make is not to the
greatest thing they desire to do or be; instead they burden it
with defenses and make it the least, the denied. For some
people, including vegetarians, they themselves might be the
"least" they need to consider: Not valuing their own
incredible, beautiful selves enough to create a practice that
restores them. For nonvegetarians, the least may be the
conscious choices they make about food.

We have learned well how to restrict our spirit's longing.
It inhabits the least space we allow it. But we need not be stuck
with the conditioned mind's approach.

**Treat yourself to a delicious vegetarian meal at
your favorite restaurant.**

The least points to the most.

If you already are a vegetarian, and this is your path, then your least must point to the most valued, using vegetarian consciousness to examine not only your food choices but your personal choices (are you taking care of yourself?) and your interpersonal choices (cultivating generosity and compassion toward others).

What are the ways in which you take care of yourself?

When you reverse direction, can you discover the gravitational pull of the "least"?

When we make the "least" in our lives a denied part of our lives, everything becomes anxiety and control, to cover or reduce the insignificant into the nonexistent. Yet, the least will not go away, and it will try to get out. Indeed, one small sense or experience of it may be enough to make you throw the entire hierarchy you have structured for yourself into the air and see what it is like when it rolls down the hill.

Notice how things roll today: Marbles, round stones, wheels. And you?

In bringing the least in line with "the most," there is an
explosion of positive energy.

For a time in my own evolution, the "least" important thing—that which I didn't do—was to eliminate eggs and cheese from my diet. "I am doing enough," I declared to myself (a declaration familiar to all of us!) I had cut down my use of them, but I still rationalized not eliminating them, "I can't expect any more of myself." But still there was the tug. No matter how I tried to minimize it, what I had made the least was tugging at my thread. My spiritual practice made it clear that, indeed, I could expect more of myself. When I finally eliminated eggs and dairy from my diet, I didn't experience depression, anxiety, or unhappiness; indeed, these were the feelings that came up because I didn't bring the least in line with the most. Instead, I experienced an explosion of energy and joy. All the energy the mind had used making excuses and my body had used in being disconnected was united and available to me in a positive way. The least asks us for integration.

Buy a plant for your house. As you water it, see your least becoming connected to the most.

We take that next step with complete compassion for ourselves.

We don't use our compassion to cover a frozenness that keeps us from our next step. The mind is always going to generate excuses, because that is one aspect of the mind. We have to help place the mind within a different context. With compassion, we can do this.

Explore aromatherapy and select one essential oil that could enrich your life.

*Recognize frozenness: If you are frozen or blocked, that
is where you are.*

We are changing a pattern in our life: Being blocked is
where the old and new hit up against one another. Realizing
one is blocked or frozen in place is a gift of discovery, for it's
here that the next stage of growth is meant to happen. The
unconscious wants truth, the truth is in your frozenness.
Excuses may keep us from encountering this frozenness.

Watch an ice cube melt.

In the spiral dance of our life, if we don't handle resistance the first time we encounter it, it'll be there again as we spiral around.

Resistance will halt our momentum toward inner growth until we stop and greet it and become friends with it. Rather than judging a blockage, ask what it has to teach you. Let it speak to you. It is telling you where you are; it is speaking of desire and fear, of hurts and hopes. The blockage forces us to confront what we are avoiding. It is saying, "The next stage of growth is meant to happen here."

Be thankful for someone who has been generous in spirit with you. They have helped you grow.

Begin again.

When you fail to keep your promises, no matter how little, begin again. And then, if necessary, begin again. Don't hold on to regret, but acknowledge you are not where you wanted to be. Accepting where we are is a component of any spiritual practice. By beginning again we learn to love our limitations. When we begin again, we are able to say, "This is where I am." Such honesty offers healing because it starts with the present moment.

Start a box or bag today for donations to a local charity. Begin again by assessing your own closet.

When growth occurs, it is usually because of a second chance.

Sometimes we know ourselves so well we can seize that first opportunity for change. But most of us do not know ourselves well enough to grab the first chance as soon as it appears. It is when we give ourselves the second chance to change that we can often seize it, because we have lived with not changing. We know it from the inside. We know what the opportunity to change felt like and we know what it felt to look the other way. Regret, frustration, sadness, bitterness invade us. Then we realize we're only one step from this inner self. This time, each movement forward feels good because we know what it felt like not to move at all.

Are you one step from a second chance?

Second chances are more flexible; they acknowledge that
what was negative can be made positive.

When we give ourselves a second chance in the vegetarian process, we feel a release of energy. We know what it felt like not to move at all; now we feel movement. We have acted on deeper connections, and these connections will grow and continue to inform us and lead us. This process is not only something occurring in the visible world; it is not only that we fix vegetable chili instead of traditional chili. The step into this commitment immerses us in an invisible network that becomes available to be experienced as we cook, eat, and share food. It arises through the positive energy we bring to our eating practice.

Take the time to make an appointment for your annual physical.

Instead of guilt, begin again.

By beginning again, you stop yourself from worrying about not being where you want to be and gently bring yourself back to the center. This is not guilt. Guilt makes you the object upon which you are imposing change rather than the subject open to change. Repetitive guilt tells you you cannot change. It stubbornly forces you to worry about not changing instead of doing it. Repetitive guilt pools in the place where second chances could grow. We simply have to change our focus.

Do a little skywriting today: Create castles in the air, throw caution to the wind, get inspired. Where can you begin again?

You know you need a second chance if your relationship to food is filled with judgment issues—"shoulds" and "don'ts."

We may be so busy controlling things that we can't take that chance. But there is nothing like seizing a second chance to give us faith in others. This is because we have acted upon our faith in ourselves.

Throw away all lists and shoulds and just live for today.

What Is Hard?—Part One.

Remember the excuses we all give about not changing? One of the most common is, "It's too hard." We're not talking about solidity here, that unbending quality that makes it difficult to change. We need to approach ease and difficulty with a different attitude. Hard is a relative term. If it is our work, and meant to be our work, "hard" has nothing to do with it. Is it your next step or not?

Watch a community of ants in motion. Try and imagine what it would be like to be an ant.

Loving something hard or difficult is a stretch.

The act of stretching stimulates our spiritual muscles just as stretching tones our physical muscles. Like a twist, which nourishes the intervertebral discs in the spine—pulpy pads that have no direct blood supply of their own and depend on our movements to nourish them—we are nourishing a part of us we do not usually nourish.

Stand and shift your attention to your spine. Straighten your back and feel yourself moving freely from this posture. Carefully twist to one side and then the other. Let your spine be nourished.

What seems "hard" may not be the act itself but the act of focusing attention.

Focus allows for expanding our self. It gives us a place to stand, and once we are standing, we can grow. Focus aligns purpose and desire. By focusing, we bring our mind into the foundation of our life and being. Becoming a vegetarian, we bring our mind to this practice. We can say, "I will experience this. This discomfort of not being able to eat these [___], I can experience this if it means that in this act I crystallize a desire to connect to other beings, to love them and the Earth and myself." And then, we realize discomfort or hardness is sometimes the way the conditioned mind interprets awareness.

Remind yourself, "It is never too late."

Making the least the most is the final piece in the puzzle.

To feel whole we have to bring all of ourselves to our lives, and whatever it is we haven't integrated into our lives—the least—is keeping us from being whole. By hiding (no matter how unconsciously) that final piece of the puzzle inside us, we're effectively saying, "There is a part of myself that doesn't need to be examined, doesn't need to be brought to light. I prefer not to know this part of me." When the least points to the most, we then achieve wholeness. We don't have to deny any relationships in our daily actions. We don't have to deny our own wild and precious life or the lives of the pigs, rabbits, chicks, or the cows. Instead of being shut off from others, connectedness with others is extended. We acknowledge the wholeness of animals, and in doing so, we move toward achieving our own wholeness.

If you don't go to restaurants because they serve dead rabbits or dead veal calves on their menu, write to them and tell them why you don't go to their restaurant.

*Spiritual vegetarianism is neither joyless nor
doctrinaire, neither spartan nor puritan.*

Food habits are the epitome of inculturation. We take
food in, transforming it from something outer to something
inner. We take in society's teaching in every bite. The teachings
are about compartmentalization: The pleasure and enjoyment
of food is unrelated to any ethics of eating. Anyone who
believes otherwise is viewed as joyless and rigid. Such a
stereotype is a sign that the conditioned mind of culture is
dragging its stone. There is little understanding of the joy that
comes form releasing the stone of cultural conditioning. And
there may be little appreciation that "new" or different foods
can be delicious and nourishing. But a next step can reveal
this.

**Focus on a favorite taste. What gives it such
mouth-feel?**

When we stop making excuses, and make the least the most, we experience abundance, plentifulness in life and living.

Living from a place of abundance occurs because we have discovered the abundance within. We have broken through resistance, and taken that next step. We let the conditioned mind do its thing, and we don't criticize; we celebrate its own abundance. But we know there is more. Our next step has revealed this! And we begin to cultivate or extend a spiritual practice because we've discovered that something internal has shifted—we are good, worthy, and whole. We don't feel cheated or reduced; instead, we feel expansion. Our next step has catalyzed this growth. The abundance of the plant world reflects our own inner abundance. Our next step uncovers what is within. Celebrate! For now we are feasting on life.

Plan a menu that uses different parts of plants. For instance: spinach (leaves), carrots (root), celery (stems), rice or corn (seeds), fruits and flowers.

The universe is in this peach before me.

The English poet William Blake wrote about seeing the world in a grain of sand.

In the beak of the finch, naturalist Charles Darwin perceived a world of evolution.

Yogis see the universe in the body.

This peach contains the sun, the rain, the dirt, the labor, the harvest. Biting into this mushroom, eating this plum. Right now, I am bringing that world within.

Yes, eat the peach. Restore the universe.

Yes, eat a peach.

There is an entire world awaiting our exploration in one bite of a peach.

There is fullness in every action, in the slicing and eating of a peach. Each moment is new. Abundantly new! With thoughtful curiosity and thankful attentiveness, we can tune into a world rich in natural vitality. We can taste life in just this way, bringing our full attention to it.

Bite into a piece of fruit and ask yourself, "What's going on in my mouth?"

The peach tells you, "You are alive!"

More than anything I know, I know this: The experience of quieting the mind's fears, and finding goodness in the process and goodness in oneself and goodness in a peach, is one process and it is available to everyone, including you right now. You are alive!

Count your blessings. Yes, list the blessings of being alive in your journal or in a letter to yourself.

What is Hard?—Part Two.

When someone says, "Isn't it hard to be a vegetarian?", my response is, "It would be harder for me to live with the knowledge that I failed to act than it is to live with the consequences of having acted."

What have you dismissed as too hard? Can you re-encounter it with a sense of opportunity?

Vegetarianism is an unspoken prayer for animals in one's
life, "I will not forget you."

"Don't you want a piece of that [___]?" the mind asks you
at a celebration.

"No, I don't," another part of you says.

"It looks pretty good," the mind beckons.

"It has [meat, eggs, milk] in it," another part of you says.

"So what?" the mind queries.

"I am perfectly happy knowing I can make a good vegan
[___]," you tell it. "I can make one when I get home if I want
to," you remind it. "You are only part of who I am. There is
something more important here. I am not going to let you
determine who I am."

"Are you sure?" the mind responds. "That [___] looks
pretty good."

"Yes, but it exists because of the suffering of animals. To
eat this piece of [___] implicates me in that system."

"You've got me on that," it concedes and moves its
attention elsewhere.

**Notice when you encounter animals during your
day today.**

To be grounded in one's community is to know how to identify where suffering is happening and what to do to transform this suffering.

Identifying suffering and knowing what to do is, in itself, a spiritual practice. But it is a fragmented one if your spiritual practice does not enable you to be at home with yourself, loving yourself enough to care about your own suffering.

Write an activist you admire and thank them for their activism.

I am eating with love and compassion for myself and for the animals.

Compassion is the ability to ask what someone is going through and to hear the answer. Nonviolence is in the hearing and also in the responding. Nonviolence is the ability to do something concrete when, in response to the question, "What are you going through?" we hear the answer, "I am suffering." Nonviolence is an intuition that one of our purposes on Earth is to reduce rather than increase harm.

Reflect on the meaning of nonviolence. What does that word conjure up for you?

For there to be compassion, there must be awareness.

For there to be awareness, we have to feel comfortable with our feelings.

To be comfortable with our feelings, we have to feel comfortable with our bodies.

To feel comfortable with our bodies, we have to have compassion for ourselves.

Ask yourself: What am I feeling right now?
 Is there any tightness, sharpness anywhere?
 Am I holding my breath or breathing?
 Am I tense or anxious?
 Is there something you need to change about the way you are sitting or standing right now?

We come from generations of rice pullers.

Near the village of Chaohwa in China, there lived a farmer named Liu. He was always impatient and in a hurry, and he always urged others to go faster. He was not only impatient with people; he was impatient with his rice. One growing season, he saw that everyone else's rice was growing more than four inches, whereas his rice was only two inches high at the most. Troubled by this, he tossed sleeplessly. Finally he awoke and recognized his purpose: He would help his rice grow. That day, all day long, he pulled slightly on the stalks of rice, and although weary and worn from his labor he was happy. The next day, he applied himself to his task again. But, on the third day, to his horror before him lay a ruined field. He had uprooted his rice.

Rice pulling is very hard work! Many of us know that firsthand. The rice pullers' mottoes are, "Trust nothing." "Move things along." But this is only our conditioning, our training, and we can change.

Think about situations that make you feel impatient. What might they be teaching you?

Rice pullers learn how not to trust our inner selves.

We know how to walk quickly and how to pull at things. We know ruined fields—we have caused them and we are them. We don't know how to let the process pull at us. This is where we have to begin—learning to trust our inner selves and our own innate ability to grow.

Bend down and feel some dirt between your hands. Does it feel healthy or not? If not, what does that make you feel?

It is necessary to cultivate the ability to ask ourselves what we ourselves are going through.

Ask yourself, "What am I feeling? What am I going through?" and answer these questions honestly. If the answer is that you yourself are suffering, then you, too, are a rice puller, and need to find out why and what you can do about it.

Ask yourself, "What am I feeling?" Answer in your journal.

We rice pullers are grasping toward some goal, some image of ourselves that tells us that who we are, here and now, is incomplete.

We believe we must do something to achieve satisfaction and completion. Usually, once we've done what we think we must, we discover yet another thing that must done. We are on an escalator of expectations that never delivers us to stable ground, but keeps us focused outward and upward. We're pulling ourselves out of the ground, out of being grounded. So we're not only the pullers, we're also the rice.

Today, resist the urge to criticize yourself and others.

We need the good soil of compassion for ourselves.

We need to recognize that we will grow at our own pace. We need our breath to rain oxygen into our blood and keep our cells fed. We need the sunlight of compassion and nonviolence for us to grow our roots and strengthen ourselves.

What can you do to love your body today?

A journal is a promise to oneself, "I matter."

Keeping a journal is both a method of self-exploration and self-affirmation, "I was here yesterday, I am here today, I will be here tomorrow." Keeping a journal is both a promise to your self and a keeping of that promise.

In your journal be "slovenly, headlong, impulsive, honest," as writer Brenda Ueland suggests. Don't judge your journal keeping, instead dance with your pen in your journal.

Compassion and nonviolence are the processes for growing rice.

When you are on the outside of them, compassion and nonviolence are experienced as concepts, only disembodied philosophical topics. But there is an alternative way to see them. You can live them. They are actions. They are the processes for growing rice—of letting things come up of their own accord.

Read a favorite poem or passage aloud today to yourself. Let your voice be heard.

I try to be compassionate because I know I suffer, and so does everyone else.

We suffer because we cling and cannot accept the truth of impermanence. We suffer because we're human. Like rice pullers, always striving to force ourselves to *be* different or *do* something, we make our own feelings unimportant and meaningless.

As rice pullers, we can't be compassionate toward our own suffering, but we can learn to replace this objectification with compassion. Nonviolence is the way to respond to yourself as you become aware of your sufferings: Do not try to uproot them.

Before speaking (or acting), take the time to ask yourself, "Will this thought (or action) increase suffering?"

The processes of developing compassion for yourself and being nonviolent are intertwined.

As you develop compassion for yourself you can see how you're violent toward yourself. As your capacity for compassion increases, your ability to see the ways you're violent toward yourself increases. Once you've developed that ability to be nonviolent to yourself, you can bring it to others. Only then can nonviolence become truly your response to the suffering of others.

Today, call and check on someone you have been thinking about.

If you are like me, your ways of denying yourself compassion might not be readily apparent.

What we most need to see we cannot necessarily see. We can never look in the mirror and know actually what we look like. As long as you are seeing with your own eyes, you can never actually see your own eyes. Spiritual practices are the closest thing to seeing your eyes with your own eyes. Then we can see how we are violent toward ourselves. And when we understand how we've been violent toward ourselves, we can actively choose a different way. If we do not make our unconscious acts of self-violence conscious, we cannot choose to be nonviolent.

Ask yourself how you are violent with yourself. Listen to what you have to say.

Our own animal bodies matter.

"The animals and the earth need me," vegetarians and animal activists say. "I can't slow down. There is so much suffering! I am needed, right now!" It is true. There is much suffering, incalculable suffering. However, we suffer too. Our own animal bodies matter.

Be attentive to your body for a few minutes. Where do you feel tight or heavy? Slowly breathe into that space and imagine yourself releasing.

Nonviolence toward ourselves begins when we decide not to force or judge but to listen and love ourselves.

What if we realized we are complete as we are, right now? What if the gifts we have, of living and being able to care, of loving and being able to receive love, exist within us right now? Another book, another successfully argued legal case, another year of teaching or plumbing or engineering—none of these will take us closer to our goal of loving ourselves or others, because we are measuring ourselves from without rather than from within. We think we're completed by something outside ourselves, and in our attempts to achieve that—whether it's recognition or success or a degree—we often have to cut ourselves off from the needy individual inside of us who desires this recognition or success.

Is there a dream character you would like to get to know? "Talk" with them in your journal. What part of you might they represent?

To be nonviolent toward yourself is to care about how you are experiencing your life.

To answer questions about your own suffering, you have to be aware of your feelings. Such awareness is not easy. Most of us have been taught to repress our feelings or, failing that, to belittle them. As a result we objectify our feelings, saying, "It's only...." But we need to counter such conditioning. And we can.

Ask yourself, "What are my wounds, and how have I tried to heal them? How am I suffering?"

*When we feel compassion for ourselves, we are careful
with ourselves.*

We have to love and care about ourselves, and be attuned
to what we are experiencing. This is why we cultivate the
spiritual discipline of attention. Attention is not a clinging, it
is an openness; not an opinion, but an invitation. It does not
legislate or dictate, it welcomes. It asks, "What am I feeling?"
It asks not only, "What am I going through?" but, "What am
I making myself go through?" Only when we are aware of our
feelings can we replace objectification with compassion.

**Ask yourself, "What am I making myself go
through?"**

What is unresolved in our lives doesn't need to be frightening to us.

If you think, "I don't know what is happening to me," that announces, "*Something* is happening to me!" And that's good! You might not understand what is happening, but at least you are aware that you are experiencing a process of happenings!

Before you go to sleep tonight, stretch your body as long as possible. Feel your body relaxing into sleep.

Love yourself.

In order to recreate your relationship with your self, you have to nurture all of yourself in order to nurture your inner self. If we don't take care of ourselves, we cannot really care about and for others. Transformative power comes from saying, "I must take care of myself."

Do you have a sacred space in your house? Create a space if you don't have one—a special, nurturing corner or part of a room where you can retreat and take care of yourself and your spirit.

Don't force.

The word compassion contains the word compass. In caring about ourselves, we begin to set a compass within ourselves. This involves recognizing how we are rice pullers toward our own selves. Ask yourself, "What am I making myself go through? Am I relentless, demanding, product-oriented? How do I encounter my own relentlessness?"

Check in: Are you writing in your journal?

The difference between violence and nonviolence.

Violence often focuses on the product, "I need to get this done." Nonviolence focuses on the process, "I need to respect myself and others."

Stop to share a few words with service people or to someone you don't normally talk to but whom you often come in contact with.

Sometimes we must be fallow ground so that at other times we can be the harvest.

We cannot grow rice in the same place all the time. Yet, many of us find it hard to accept the need to rest, even when our soil is exhausted. Do you resist resting and equate resting with passivity or confuse resting with being neglectful? Do you think that if you relax you are neglecting something? You are neglecting something when you don't rest—yourself. We need the rest in the word restoration.

Take a moment to think about what the word "rest" means to you.

Doing "nothing" is sometimes the something we need to be doing.

When we are resting and feel as though nothing is happening, growth is happening. Rest allows us to become spiritually aligned. Rest is an opportunity to be receptive. It is essential. Rest is nonviolence toward ourselves.

Give yourself permission to do nothing.

As we try to stop being violent toward ourselves we can then follow the process.

We learn how to trust our inner selves and how to move forward from that trust without anxiety, knowing that this is what we need to be doing. We embrace the process.

Spend a moment today thinking of someone to thank. Remind yourself to do the same tomorrow.

*A spiritual person allows the spontaneous and the good
to arise within her or him.*

Through a spiritual practice we experience the radical
notion that we are each good and worthy of care. We begin
with ourselves, discovering the goodness of creation and the
goodness of each of us. We then desire to extend the good.

Develop your own helping rituals.

By taking care of ourselves we can ask how we can help others.

Authentic nonviolent living empowers us to love ourselves. And in doing so we can love others.

Donate to your local animal shelter—blankets, cat litter, cat, dog, or rabbit food, old towels.

A spiritual practice creates inner space.

Living in the world today is often a process of constricting energy. When one is tense, the muscles contract, closing off and blocking energy flow. Like a detour, this reroutes energy, so that it spills into dreams and journals. Spiritual practice releases the energy, allowing the muscles and heart to relax.

Are there any places in your head, face, neck, or shoulders where you feel tension or pain? Breathe deeply and as you exhale say to yourself, "I am feeling relaxed."

"We are every part of a dream."

This guide to dream interpretation provides yet another way of approaching the concept and experience of nonduality. When I dream of a monster attacking me, I immediately identify with the "me" in the dream and I'm frightened. However, although I'm less likely to see it, I'm also the monster. A part of me is frightening! And the "monster me" is trying to tell me something.

Recall a nightmare and ask yourself, "What part of me was frightening in the dream?"

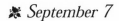
The Chase.

When we have dreams in which someone or something frightening is chasing us, the chasing is a part of us we're avoiding. We can run from it all we want, but it will be there again, chasing us the next night or the next. Until we turn and face the threatening individual or monster, we won't be reunited with what we are avoiding, and our dreams of being chased won't stop. This is the lesson of being blocked.

Write about a dream that was frightening.

The world in the dream is us.

When we see ourselves as every part of the dream, we can discover meanings we might have missed otherwise. We are not passive in the dream, even if our dream "I" is. We make everything happen. Through a specific dream analysis, you may realize you are making choices and be liberated to make different choices. As we consciously practice recognizing how we are everything in a dream, we are taught a lesson in nonduality.

What choices are being made in your dreams? Who is making them? What part of you do they represent?

*When you begin to be aware of your relentless
expectations and try to replace them with compassion
for yourself, you discover how much space is inside you.*

When you became aware of how you are violent to
yourself and begin to cultivate an interior nonviolence, you
discover the goodness within yourself. With more interior
space, you can embrace what happens, welcome it and
assimilate it. You are not trapped by it. You are not
claustrophobic inside. Instead, you experience the depth of
relationships.

**Reclaim your space: Light incense, open a
window, play your favorite music, breathe deeply.**

By having compassion for ourselves, we transform a cup of water into an ocean.

Sharon Salzberg observes that a tablespoon of salt in a cup of water will taste different from a tablespoon of salt in an ocean. The salt is the same, but the amount of water is different. We are the water. When anger enters a more confined body, whether physically or emotionally, it is like a tablespoon of salt in a cup of water. But through spiritual practice, we increase within, and when the salt of bitterness, frustration, or anger is mixed in, we realize we have become like the ocean.

Imagine a positive way of handling anger in your life.

When things are too "heavy," there is no space for absorbing anything.

When anger enters a confined, tight body, it bounces from tightness to tightness. We know only tight muscles and density. A clear body opens channels for energy. When anger enters a relaxed body, a body at peace, there is nothing hard to give it a bounce. A body that has space inside it is light: Nothing is too "heavy" for us. We can allow ideas and feelings in and not try to block the energy those ideas and feelings generate. Spaciousness of the body, openness, and lightness are interrelated.

With your back straight, sigh deeply. As the air leaves your lungs, let out a sound. Don't consciously inhale. Just await inhalation in its own time. Repeat.

Space is what you create within yourself by consciously trying to empty yourself of desires and simply stay present to the moment.

Freedom of spaciousness:
Emptying myself of desires
desires destroy the present moment
desires are substitutes for experience
desires make me "full" when I want to be empty.

Don't plan; allow your day—or part of it—to unfold. What do you feel?

day · 1 ·

Equally empty means empty of attachment.

I do not have to be attached to what happened yesterday; I do not have to be worried about what is going to happen tomorrow. Equally empty means I am committed to a process, not a product.

Say something out lou... or sing a song of praise... of a process of creation.

being prese...
let go of E...
it will unfo...

in the process

⟨→ ⤊ ⇄
/ | \

FEEL ⌣ *birds*

JAN 1

V. is an acknowledge-
ment of relationships:
↔ my choice of food
+ bodys health;
↔ me + people,
animals
↔ my actions +
earths health.

World is organized
to keep ~~you~~ meateater
" " me from acknowl-
relationships.

Equally empty means begin again.

Let go of the past, embrace the present.

Equally empty means the past does not determine the present.

Equally empty means I can empty myself of excuses.

We are all equally empty, empty of yesterdays, and empty of tomorrows.

Look at the stars and experience this moment.

The Equally Empty Meditation.

We each are equally in need of love, equally the focus of love. Each of us is also on a path of awakening to our Buddha nature, which is a way of saying, "I am awake. I follow awareness."

Begin this meditation by naming yourself
> **[your name], equally empty.**
> **[your name], equally to be loved.**
> **[your name], equally a coming Buddha (or equally awakening).**

Extending the Equally Empty Meditation. (see previous page)

Then name the people with whom you live.

Name people who you are thinking about, or whose afflictions you've become aware of.

If you have a particularly strong feeling about someone, name that person.

[_____], **equally empty.**

[_____], **equally to be loved.**

[_____], **equally a coming Buddha (or equally awakening).**

By having compassion for ourselves, we create space inside.

Once that space is created, we can invite others inside: Our partners, children, parents, every being on the Earth. Compassion flows naturally to others because we have space inside to care about them all.

Find out about and support a local animal advocacy group.

*In being able to acknowledge life's up and downs, you
can be more life-affirming.*

Vegetarian feelings are anchored within the inner space
we have created. Vegetarian spirituality affirms to animals, "I
have enough room inside me to include concern for you."
Spiritual practices make that statement possible. They are the
process of creating and maintaining that spaciousness.

**Before eating today, remind yourself, "I have
enough room inside me to include concern for
animals."**

We are caught in clinging.

Because I have compassion for my own suffering, because I understand that I cling to things in an attempt to deny impermanence, I can understand that you cling to things. What we cling to may be very different. But through clinging, we freeze the part of us that knows about impermanence, and empower the part that resists impermanence.

With water soluble markers, draw on your feet. Enjoy the design and, as you wash it off, think about impermanence.

Compassion for others is nonviolence in action.

The three steps—attention, love, and don't force—that form the core of self-care are the platform on which we craft compassion for others. If I feel compassion for you, I won't be inflexible, demanding, or firm. I won't approach you with ultimatums. I will want to know where you are now: What your hopes and, more importantly, what your fears are.

Share a piece of knowledge with someone without trying to show off.

A Breathing Partners Meditation for the Autumn Equinox.

Inhaling, I breathe deeply.

Exhaling, I acknowledge myself.

Inhaling, I feel the breath move through me.

Exhaling, I share my breath with you, plants and animals.

Inhaling, I know that you share your breath with me.

Exhaling, I acknowledge you, plants and animals.

Inhaling, I feel the breath move through me.

Exhaling, I know that breath moves through you, too.

Inhaling, I breathe deeply.

Exhaling, I breathe with you.

Sit still. If you feel your back slump, sit on a pillow or a chair. Repeat each couplet several times, feeling yourself becoming more centered. Continue through the meditation, devoting about fifteen minutes to it.

Spiritual vegetarianism is not about rice pulling.

Ironically, it is in their relationship with others that vegetarians are often experienced as violent or aggressive, as rice pullers. If a nonvegetarian thinks I am saying, "Why aren't you a vegetarian?", then I'm on the outside of her or his process and can only be experienced as judging her or him. This causes the nonvegetarian to think that vegetarians are rigid and judgmental. When we are self-righteous rice pullers, we do not offer any empty spaces to someone else; we are too filled. The interaction cannot work because each individual path is blocked by our unyielding presence.

As you walk today, look at the sidewalk or other areas of concrete: Are there signs that plant life is breaking through? Can this be a metaphor for your life?

Because we're all related, our compassion for ourselves creates the ability to feel compassion for the suffering of others.

From this sense of relatedness, we also encounter the desire to relieve suffering rather than inflict harm. We bring this compassion to our activism, by asking of our activism: Does it cause fear? Does it objectify individuals? Does it fail to acknowledge their feelings or their life? Does it use humor? Does it acknowledge commonalties or shared intentions?

Today, weigh and measure everything you say. Don't speak until you have to. What does it mean to be silenced?

Lightness of spirit frees us to encounter others with less gravity.

When we are able to feel less seriousness about ourselves, we release the solidity that makes us as unbending with others as we are with ourselves. We need not be impatient rice pullers toward others, we can be generous. We can let rice grow.

Plant a tree.

Generosity says, "You can pass this way too."

Generosity frees the "I," rather than freezing it. Rather than "maybe" or "no," generosity says yes.

Say "yes" to something today that you would usually say no to.

The process you are undergoing is one of widening: In ability and in flexibility.

A window frame, a book on a bookshelf, an upside-down capital letter "T"—whenever a horizontal line meets a vertical line, you can be reminded of the benefits of spiritual practice: You experience abundance within yourself and without. You are not so "narrow." You are not so threatened by things. Your "narrow-mindedness" is transformed.

Check in: Have you made promises? Did you keep them?

Generosity is not controlling; it thinks the best.

Your spiritual practices allow you to feel your way through an experience and to allow another to do the same. You can be patient, more receptive, and more able to bring more things into your life. This, too, is generosity. It is our presence, our attention, to what is going on.

Open the door for someone today. Let someone else go first.

Generosity lets rice grow.

Generosity is not passive. It has to prepare the field, remove the weeds, bring water. This is what activism does. And, it is an activism that arises from a feeling of generosity toward ourselves and others. Likewise, spiritual practice does not pull us away from this world; it equips us to move into the world. In every interaction, we are able to draw upon more of us. When I am focused, I can process information more quickly. Being grounded as an activist, I can stand my ground. I touch the earth as I work on behalf of the Earth. I don't lose that elemental connection. If generosity tramples the rice as it tends the field, it has lost sight of its relationship to the Earth.

Free associate on the meaning of earth to you.

The fruits of a spiritual practice are that you can be a nonanxious person with yourself.

People share their anxieties with me when they describe why they aren't vegetarians or why they haven't adopted a spiritual practice. I was thinking about this when I went for a walk with my friend Pat, a professor of pastoral care. She was discussing an upcoming visit that she expected would be stressful. As we walked through the fall leaves, she sighed and said, "My students are always quoting me, 'As Professor Davis says, "Be the nonanxious person." ' "

She paused. "I wish I could be the nonanxious person when my friend is here."

"Nonanxious person," I said. "What an interesting concept. What does it mean exactly?"

"It's the role of the counselor, according to family therapy," Pat replied. "The counselor is the nonanxious person." So is a spiritual person.

Give thanks for your friends.

*We vegetarians and spiritual practitioners can be the
nonanxious person because we've learned not to be
afraid of following the process.*

We can be aware of our energy because we're willing to
follow it. We're willing to take maximum responsibility for our
own emotional well being and our life. This, too, is touching
the process. What energy is before me? What energy is within
me? Where does my energy direct me? We follow the process.

I release stress healthily by . . . .

Anxiety pretends it is an authentic feeling; in fact, it kills what is authentic.

Anxiety is nervous and unanchored energy, a drumroll of worries and excuses. Anyone who is anxious knows its familiar signs. Anxiety is words in your head, tightness in your belly, and no connection with your energy center. Anxiety takes one's feeling of freedom and reduces it to "decisions." Anxiety is energy that short-circuits itself, causing our energy to spin round and round, making its focus smaller and smaller.

Become aware of how you feel anxiety. In what part of your body does anxiety express itself— stomach ache, nausea, pain in the neck, a gripping in the stomach, hair rising, a sinking in the stomach?

Anxiety is only superficially about inner processes.

Anxiety takes all the inner energy and focuses it on an object instead of on a process. Anxiety is misfocused energy before the act. It is the experience of having expectations and fearing they won't be met. Anxiety divides inner energy; peace is connected to it.

Become aware of how you know that something is true. Do you feel bubbling energy, blood rushing to the face, tears of happiness, movement of energy up the spine?

When we touch the process, we release anxiety and heal our anxious self.

Anxiety fears loss—that aching, painful, hollow feeling where something should be. Anxiety often keeps us from changing. Anxiety holds on rather than releasing. The anxious person asks, "Who will take care of me?" The answer is, "I must take care of myself." The answer is, "I am worth taking care of."

Take some time today to be really silly. Roll around on the floor. Jump up and down. Dance a lot. Make faces in the mirror.

Anyone who is an activist should examine how she experiences herself as solid versus fluid.

Often we are most solid when we are confrontational, and we need to ask what we gain from being confrontational. If we are merely confirming our own sense of righteousness, then we are being solid. When something solid meets another solid, there's little movement. We need to be a catalyst for growth, and this is best achieved by being fluid.

Free associate on the meaning of water to you.

As we begin to bring a desired part of us into existence,
we discover a feeling of regret.

Regret is a sign that we are attached to outcome rather than process. We judge the self *then*, rather than accepting the self *now*. This judgment means we don't accept the gifts of the present moment.

Reread your journal(s) and learn about who you have been and who you are becoming.

Regret is judgment's press secretary.

Regret imposes a retroactive "should." Regret is closed-circuit energy; it looks to external causes and effects. Regret assumes blame. Regret is learning the wrong lesson.

Think about what happened today. Was there anything you regret? Think to yourself why you did what you did the way you did, and how you might have done it differently. Are there any lessons you can draw?

Regret occurs instead of receptivity.

While receptivity moves the process, regret halts the energy, labels it, and judges it. Regret attaches itself to the past as a way to mourn the self we didn't become, rather than become the self we can become now. Our past flails us with failure, rather than revealing the steps that led us to the point of discovery. Regret is the rope around the stone.

Move your shoulders and as you do see yourself releasing the "shoulds" in your life.

Like regret, a dream pattern that appears semi-fixed is telling us something.

Through dream themes that repeat themselves over and over again, regret may be working within us and pointing to a quality we want to achieve but that we have failed to integrate. The repetitious nature of the dream theme suggests very strongly that something of priority in our life is basically the same as it was the last time we dreamed this dream. We might think we've changed, but the recurring dream is telling us otherwise. There may have been obvious developments and changes, but the dream is directing our attention to what has not changed. What is triggering the repetition of the dream?

Take the time to write down key elements in a dream that repeats itself. Ask yourself, why am I dreaming this dream? Write the answer with your nondominant hand.

While regret is a sign we're on a desired path, we must fling it aside to move forward.

Regret acknowledges we've experienced a sense of change and then either wants to speed it up or cling to the past ("I can't expect any more from myself"). The past has led us to this moment—one that need not be determined by the past. We are free from clinging to decisions made in the past that prevent us from changing.

Eat/drink something you didn't like as a child. Maybe you've changed.

Honor desperation.

There is this to say for desperation: It is a great catalyst. When you realize you've been living someone else's life and denying inner yearnings, this discovery can propel you forward. When someone exclaims, "I can't go on like this!", she gives herself the ability to change. The desperation arises with the realization that she isn't doing what she wants to do, that she is living in or clinging to the past. Or else desperation announces, "I have been living with expectations, not practices." If you are feeling desperate, then change one thing and only one thing, but change it now. Then you will experience what it means to live in the present.

Today, change one thing about your life.

Breath is life.

We rarely concentrate our awareness on our breathing. Since we take about 20,000 breaths a day, we are fortunate the activity does not require our conscious attention! The yogis say that air is our food. We can fast for days, but we cannot skip breathing. Breath marks our beginning and its cessation announces our ending: it is life. If we stop breathing, we die.

Notice your breathing. Is it shallow or deep? From the chest or lower? Do you breath from your mouth or your nose?

Prana *is the universal life force that we share with all other beings.*

The Sanskrit word *prana* literally means "breathing forth," but it has come to represent the universal life force. *Prana* is at work in our respiration, our circulation, our digestion, and in all body processes. *Prana* is at work within... and without.

Free associate on the meaning of air to you.

Breath unites us human and nonhuman animals: We all breathe.

Prana means spirit or consciousness; in Greek the term is *pneuma*, literally breath, wind, spirit. Just as with *prana*, *pneuma* also connotes the vital spirit. In Latin, we find a similar word working at more than one level. The word *anima* means the soul, spirit, life, breath. It comes from a root word meaning to breathe. The word *animal* comes from the same root word; it is from *animalis*, living—from anima, the soul.

Give a subscription of *The Animals' Agenda* magazine (www.animalsagenda.org) to your local library.

Breathing is a process, one that is always happening now.

Breath awareness at its most basic means this: Breathing is a process, one always happening now. If my breath were only in the past tense, I wouldn't have long to live. In becoming aware of my breath, I become more fully alive. Awareness of breathing links us to the present moment.

Again, focus your mind on your breathing right now.

> **What is its quality?**
> **How rapid is it?**
> **How many breaths do you take in a minute?**

Breathing is influenced by how we live in our bodies.

If we are constricted, without a straight, lengthened spine, so is our breathing. Unfortunately, part of growing up means losing the sense of our bodies that enables natural, deep breathing. We wear tight clothes that restrict the movement of the abdomen. We sit at desks and in cars in ways that encourage slumping. We have to create the physical space to allow the breath to go deeper within us.

What position are you holding right now? Where can you feel your breath? Where don't you feel your breath?

Through breath awareness, our mind can focus on one thing.

While the mind can have more than one thought at a time, the body can only have one breath. Spiritual practices help to integrate the mind within body. Through these practices, the mind releases control and is brought into the process too. This creates a feeling of unity. Where once there was duality—mind and body—there is now no duality, or what is known as nonduality. In a state of nonduality, we experience our connectedness to every being, every part of creation.

Today, try taking three very deep, slow breaths before eating.

Nonduality is a breath away.

When body, soul, and mind are breathing with one thought, thinking with one action, and acting with one purpose, our spirit experiences connections. Joy flows from this experience of connection. It is only a breath away.

Today, breathe deeply before you speak. What do you feel?

We are the breathing partners of plants.

The guard cells are breathing. Because the guard cells breathe, we breathe. These guard cells are not within us; they are in a plant's stomata, providing openings to the atmosphere. Kidney-shaped, they face each other. The guard cells are the plant's nose and mouth. Depending upon how much fluid is in the guard cells, they inflate and deflate, allowing the opening—the stoma—to open and close. When they breathe, oxygen goes out. Our cells need this oxygen. About 20,000 times a day, our noses and mouths bring the oxygen into our lungs; the lungs pass the oxygen into the bloodstream, and this carries it to the cells. Here the oxygen nourishes and repairs our cells. The blood then carries the cells' waste product—carbon dioxide—back to the lungs, and we expire it into the air. The plants need our carbon dioxide. We are the breathing partners of plants

Be thankful for plants.

Breathing Time.

When we have had too much of something and need a break, we say we need some "breathing time." Breathing time is space to recover, to become refreshed, to start again. Breathing time helps us to experience how we are the breathing partners of plants.

Do you need breathing time in your life right now?

Breathing heals the illusion of separation.

Through breath awareness, physically and conceptually we discover how our lives are connected with our breathing partners: The plants and the other animals. When we move our breath deeper into our body, and feel it enrich the blood, feel it reach all the cells and restore them, we can find within our body a sense of the entire world.

Are you aware of air pollution issues in your community?

We have an oxygen debt to plants.

The yogis say that air is our food. Air feeds our cells, but air is food for plants in a way entirely different than it is for us. While we need both air and food, plants, on the other hand, are autotrophs. The word trophic means "of or relating to nutrition," and being autotrophic means being able to feed yourself. Plants produce their own food. From sunlight (the ultimate source of energy), carbon dioxide, and water, the biochemical reaction we know as photosynthesis occurs. Plants take the carbon dioxide we have expired and break it down. That carbon dioxide, along with energy from the sun, water, and enzymes in the plant itself, will ultimately produce the sugar molecule. When the plant needs energy, it breaks down the sugar molecule, and in the process of breaking down the sugar molecule, energy is produced. It can be used for whatever the plant needs to function or to grow. The oxygen without which we cannot live is a by-product of this process.

Ask yourself: Where are plants in my life? Do I eat them directly or indirectly. That is, do I require that plants first be consumed by animals, and then I eat the animal?

With a journal, I bring what is usually buried into the light, and examine my root structure.

Swami Sivananda Radha suggests that a daily journal is like the cross section of a tree—it records and reveals the story of our life. Drought, stunted growth, normal growth, overcrowding—all of these processes are revealed in the cross-section of a tree. My journal reveals my growth and where I have been stunted, experienced claustrophobia or a parched spirit. It asks how deeply I've placed my roots.

Check in: Are you keeping a journal? If not, begin again. If so, reread your journal and ask yourself, "Am I growing? Are my roots getting nourishment? Where is the fruit of my actions?"

The German poet and naturalist Johann Wolfgang von Goethe said that the marvel is not that an apple falls from the tree, but that a tree can grow in opposite directions at the same time.

Through spiritual practice, we grow in opposite directions at the same time—outward in ability to embrace the world's sufferings, inward to embrace our own.

Go for a "leaf walk" in your neighborhood. How many different kinds of leaves do you see?

Plants are primary producers; they rely on the sun's energy to produce their own food.

Vegetarians and herbivores are primary consumers; they rely on the plants for food. They require that less energy be exerted in the creation of their food. When we humans become secondary consumers—consumers of both plant food and animals—we construct an environment built on using energy rather than conserving it.

Sit under a tree and feel how its presence affects you.

"What about plants?"

Nonvegetarians or secondary consumers demand more of the plant world than vegetarians do. When nonvegetarians ask of the vegetarian, "Isn't the plant you're eating suffering too?", they fail to realize it is the nonvegetarian diet that requires multiple numbers of plants. Nonvegetarians are simply getting those increased numbers of plants indirectly, through feed to the animals whom they eat. The closer we are to the primary producers, the less we demand of the natural world and the more integrity we allow the planet.

Try and catch a leaf from a tree. What does it mean to fall from the tree?

*Many people have told me that they tried to be a
vegetarian once and that it didn't work.*

When they tell me "it didn't work," I try to help them to
see that the problems they encountered were teaching them
that they couldn't become a vegetarian in that way. Their
failure was an indication that they should try a different way
and give themselves a second chance.

**Try peeling the skin of a grape from its flesh
within your mouth.**

We work against ourselves in two directions simultaneously.

A tree grows in two directions at the same time. In the same way, we work against ourselves in two directions simultaneously when forests are cut down either for fodder or to make way for pastures. When we destroy trees to make way for animals who will be eaten, we decrease the ability of the planet to handle the carbon dioxide released into the air by human beings. At the same time as we decrease the number of trees that could process the carbon dioxide, we increase its production by adding more cows to the environment.

Read a newspaper or magazine article about the environment. Does it address the problem of meat eating? Write a letter of condolence, concern, or celebration in response to the article.

We all have a life force.

The question arises, "Why I should deprive others of their breaths?" In producing plants to be eaten by animals, and cutting down forests so that the animals who will be eaten have a place to live, we deny relationships. Why should I destroy my breathing partners?

Buy recycled paper; reuse paper only printed on one side; save envelopes from direct mail and reuse them.

We will breathe with you.

Breathing time is a time to remember that we're all breathing the breath of all beings. Because we are aware of you, animals, on this level—the level of being, we might think to ourselves—we choose not to use you on the level of object. We will not assume the role of secondary consumer. We will breathe with you.

Listen to the breathing of an animal.

Vegetarianism is often more like letting go.

Breathing is inhalation and exhalation. Inhalation is active; exhalation is receptive. Many people think vegetarianism is about control, but it is not. We let go of foods that we used to be attached to. We release ourselves of that attachment. Vegetarianism, like exhalation, is receptive.

What have you released, let go of in your life? If you are a nonvegetarian, is there one meat or dairy food that you can let go of? If you are a vegetarian, is there something you are aware of that you wish to release?

*The cow is complete in her existence when she is alive
and not dead.*

To approach other animals in the present moment, nondualistically, involves meeting them where they are, right now. Then we can encounter what it is that makes a cow a cow, a pig a pig, or a rabbit a rabbit: their distinctive "cowness," "pigness," or "rabbitness."

**Remember with gratitude animals who have been
in your life.**

*If our relationship to animals requires their death, we're
asking animals to meet us where we are, rather than
meeting them where they are.*

We can't experience their "cowness" in the present
moment because we're subordinating their cowness to our
desires. We hold onto the dualism: We're meat eating humans
and they're "meat" animals. A primary producer, say a peach,
can be fully "peach" and also be consumed. Its peachness does
not change. But a cow is changed into meat by ceasing to be a
cow. We turn the relationship we may have had between two
living beings into one directed only from the human level. In
doing so, we change the flow of energy.

**If you pray, pray for all beings, that their lives will
not be shortened.**

How can we change the presumption that we know the
direction of an animal's life?

Many spiritual practitioners believe that something is achieved for the cow (or pig or rabbit or fish) by being eaten. But this is an item of faith, rather than fact. It assumes we know something about cowness and pigness and rabbitness and fishness, when in fact all we can assume is that, like us, most animals do not want to be eaten.

Countdown to Thanksgiving: Plan ahead. Where are you going and what will you need?

We are not a better "chimpanzee."

We've created a hierarchy to explain our place in evolution and we survey the world from our position at the top. We see ourselves as the primary beings, while those below us are secondary. We think we can trace an ascending line of life forms that are evolving and becoming better, until the line reaches us, the human beings, better than all the rest. We judge that those nearer the base are "more primitive" than those higher up. But this pyramid results from a faulty understanding of evolution. To measure evolution by the concept of "progress" is to use a human concept as though it were a biological principle. It is not.

If your neighborhood grocery stores offer specials on animal products, suggest to them that they offer comparable savings on vegan protein products.

Vegetarianism is deeply embedded within spiritual consciousness about the interconnectedness of all life.

Spiritual practices create a sense of connectedness. Through breath awareness, individually and conceptually we discover how our lives are connected with our breathing partners: The plants and the other animals. When we use breath awareness as the guide to consider our relationships with them, we may see how using animals for food rips apart the fabric of life. Vegetarianism honors our interconnectedness.

Countdown to Thanksgiving: Write a letter to the editor describing a wonderful vegetarian Thanksgiving meal you had in the past.

The image of a tree can carry into your journal.

In your journal you can think in two directions simultaneously, balancing inner and external knowledge. You can be aware simultaneously that you are limiting yourself in some way and aware of what is happening to the trees on our planet. You can use your journal to deepen your roots, to prune activities, and to go out on a limb.

Are your roots nourishing you? Are you nourishing activism that protects trees?

*A spiritual person touches a part of him- or herself that
is not reachable in ordinary ways.*

The person without a spiritual practice may fear there is
nothing beyond the external world; or, more specifically, that
there is nothing worthy in the internal world. But so much
exists inside; keeping a journal reveals this to you. The need for
inner work leaks out in our confrontations with others if we
do not consciously allow time for ourselves. Inner work is not
passive. One's inner life is just as worthy, just as important, as
the outside life.

**With a colorful pen, sketch a picture in your
journal. Make lists, ask questions, answer
questions. Let your inner self come to the page
and play. Touch yourself through writing and
drawing.**

Our own bodies are a part of our work at this point in time.

Because we have denied so much about our bodies, including their own intelligence, our own bodies are a part of our work at this point of time. "I"—the mind—is not telling "my" body what to do. To function in that way is to continue dualisms, as though one part of me, the mind, possesses all of the body and is only in my brain and not throughout my body. Why speak of "my hamstrings," as in the sentence, "I feel tight in my hamstrings"? Instead, consciousness is in the hamstrings, the hips, and in the toes. Your breath can lead you to experience this.

Go for a walk and notice how you move through your body. Feel the different parts of your body. What does it feel like to be hand? Or leg? To be muscle? Or bone?

Through vegetarianism, you learn how to listen to your body.

Your body knows how to be vegetarian and your mind can learn the wisdom of not holding on to the permanence of old identities.

Lie in a comfortable position and listen to your body.

Vegetarianism lightens and heals the body by reducing the effects of the pull of gravity on our internal organs.

As gravity pulls on our body—and all the organs associated with digestion—meat and dairy push on them. Just as breath oxygenates the blood, vegetarianism allows for the healing and repairing of the body; vegetarianism works with the organs of the body. If we are vegetarians, our organs don't need to filter meat and its impurities. The pull of gravity is not exacerbated by the grossness/drossness of food pushing down on the organs, weighing them down. Through vegetarianism, we create the space around and in our internal organs to experience flow rather than pressure. This is why people often feel better within days of trying vegetarianism.

Countdown to Thanksgiving: Have you considered organizing a vegan meal for your friends or family?

Bodies are such miracles.

It takes time to discover the miracle of our bodies. Animals' bodies are miracles too. As we are able to touch our own bodies more deeply, and experience the miracle of them, our breath, and the world in them, we may be able to become more aware of how animals experience their bodies.

Experience the miracle of being awake. Move through your day as though it was the first time you were encountering what you encounter.

Releasing the psoas muscle is a way of touching our depth.

When we contract our muscles and teach ourselves to live with contracted muscles, we close off the ability to process fear and other emotions that are being experienced. The psoas muscle is part of a group of flexor muscles that, according to Liz Koch, "contracts whenever the fear reflex fires." The psoas muscle is an unusual muscle because it unites the upper and lower parts of our body, connecting the rib cage and trunk to the legs. It does not attach to the pelvis itself, but passes through it. It is at the core of the body. Because it is located so deeply within us, the psoas is also a metaphor for what is happening in our spiritual practice.

Look up the word "psoas" in a dictionary.

The psoas muscle requires release.

When the psoas muscle is relaxed, it can lengthen. This is especially important for activists, since protest often demands that we stand. In standing we often experience a range of emotions around the issue we're protesting and the interactions with people who disagree with us. The emotional tension from confrontation may be stored in the psoas. Unless we release that muscle, we won't release the emotional tension that keeps us frozen and frightened of ourselves and others.

Where is your psoas muscle? Close your eyes and imagine that you can see it uniting the lower and upper parts of your body.

Breathing and Fear.

In the face of the need to change, many people feel fear. What will change mean and what will it require of them? Do you know that experience? When you feel it, do you want to close down against fear and tighten? But what would happen if you loosened instead?

Breathe into your psoas muscle.

Following our fear is like viewing the (usually) invisible
root structure of a tree.

With our breath we can follow our fear rather than letting our fear make us feel afraid. We can say to the fearful part of ourselves, "Hello. Here you are again. I know you. I have seen your root structure."

In your journal, or as a letter to yourself, list all your fears. What scares you? Be honest. And then thank your fearful part of you for being honest. Breathe deeply and let your breath speak to your fears.

We don't need to expect there will be an end to fear.

There may be no ultimate resolution. But there can be a transformation in how we release the feelings of fear. As we breathe and create space inside, fear has less of a place to take root as we breathe and create space inside.

Look at your list of fears. Choose the fears that seem most pressing. Work with them. Ask them questions. Imagine them giving answers. What are they teaching you?

Fear prevents us from loving ourselves.

When a sense of danger is present, we experience fear, not anxiety; we become frightened about something or someone. If there is something dangerous threatening us, we need to determine how to respond. But often the fear response misfires. Although there is no danger, we are geared to fear. When that happens, we funnel energy into being fearful. We fear being judged and found incomplete; we fear others. We become chronically fearful.

Notice your energy—are you tired, excited, do you have sleepless nights or exhausted days? Where does your energy wish to go? How can you love yourself?

To counter fear we have to love the part of ourselves that fears.

The part of you that fears may be protecting you from something it no longer comprehends. Bringing your fears to consciousness is one way of lessening their power. Fear may be keeping you from changing.

Consciously relish a new piece of knowledge or information you received today. Consciously enjoy the process of changing. Assure yourself that changing has its own rewards.

To care for the animals through spiritual vegetarianism
is to care for myself.

By having space for animals in our hearts, we create space within our body. This is how we discover the world in our body. Through vegetarianism we do not put the world in the form of dead animals into our body. Instead, we cultivate the ability to feel the world within.

Countdown to Thanksgiving: Be aware if you are feeling grief because of the killing of turkeys. Allow yourself to feel that grief. Tell yourself that the grief is the gift of being awake.

Consciousness includes the suffering of others.

In a recent interview, a yoga teacher explained that he had once been a vegetarian, but that he now ate meat again. The difference, though, was that now he ate it with consciousness. A spiritual practice enables us to accept where we are and not legislate and judge.

Yet, whose consciousness is he talking about? Of necessity, it was his own. We cannot violate our own consciousness. But what about eating with consciousness about animals' bodies too? If through breathing and other spiritual practices we experience nonduality, can we eat only with consciousness about ourselves?

Write in your journal the early messages about food you received when you were growing up.

The conceptual flows from the perceptual.

United Poultry Concerns' founder Karen Davis takes a replica of a battery hen cage with five artificial but very realistic-looking hens crammed into it to rallies, meetings, and educational events. Each of the hens has a facial expression. People approach the cage, wondering, "Why are these chickens in there?" Perception leads the way, and then they hear the answer, "This is how ninety-five percent of the chickens who lay eggs live." Attention leads to caring, because it is clear that five hens in a battery cage causes much suffering. The individual encountering his own perceptions realizes, "Now that I've seen one bird and seeing made me understand, I do not have to see every bird to know that this should be challenged."

Countdown to Thanksgiving: Contribute to a farm sanctuary that shelters turkeys.

"Overeating is a form of stealing."

Georg Feuerstein, in explaining not stealing—one of the *yamas*, or moral principles of yoga—remarks, "Overeating is a form of stealing." Meat eating is another form of stealing. Rather than use the food resources directly, meat eating requires that food first be fed to animals. Animals then transform vegetable protein into animal protein. In choosing animalized protein, meat eaters, in a sense, are stealing the food that went into the animals.

Remember that there is joy in offering simple, good food to your guests.

We are our soul's taxidermist.

Another word for overeating is a word out of taxidermy—
"stuffing," an action that fills what is inert. The word reveals
the process of disconnection. Without attention or love, we
make our bodies receptacles for food rather than intimate
partners in eating.

**Try a different tea than you usually drink. Relish
the new.**

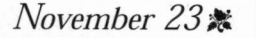

The hungering self is a suffering self.

Our inner self hungers for love and time, and needs to be treated well. If we can recognize that the hungering self in us is a suffering self, we can bring compassion to that self that is suffering and is clinging to food for solace. Often, instead, we translate the deep hungering of our souls into what we can understand: Physical hunger. When we are depressed we may think we need some chocolate, when what we really need is not chocolate but time to figure out why we're depressed. We're not integrating the hungering self into our lives; instead, we interpret its needs as cravings.

Breathe deeply and slowly before eating.

The mind holds on to the desire for old tastes because old tastes speak to an emotional/spiritual need.

When we've stuffed ourselves, the hungering self sleeps and doesn't talk to us. The hungering self knows memory—the memory of meals. It knows desire—the desire for a certain taste. It is happiest when it is eating or full. Then, it feels in control. But the hungering self doesn't deal with the consequences: Feeling bloated, hating oneself, depression. "Feed me," the hungering self demands. "I know how to handle these feelings!" And so, the endless treadmill continues. The mind holds on to the desire for old tastes because old tastes speak to an emotional/spiritual need. If that need is unaddressed, the person will remain frozen in her or his hungering patterns.

Select a famous chef. Give a donation to a vegan organization in her or his name and write them and tell him or her why you did.

To engage in stuffing down feeling, stuffing ourselves with dead foods, a part of us is dead inside, and we are inattentive.

To experience our own and others' suffering tells us we are alive inside, and that we are attentive.

Do a little "firewalking" today: Get incensed about injustice, get fired up about a project, and remind yourself not to burn out.

When Love Occurs.

Love occurs when we are able to ask what others are going through and have the space inside to hear the answer and the space to understand our relationship to that suffering. And then, because we have created space inside to hear and to understand, we act to stop the suffering.

Love is in the hearing.

Love is in the understanding.

And love is in the acting.

Ask someone what they are going through.

Identify what you are hungering for.

We may realize that we get a sense of worthiness from the foods we eat, and we think a change of diet will deny us this sense of worthiness:

We hunger for worthiness.

We may relish a hamburger, a cheese pizza.

We hunger for joy.

Eating may often be the only place where we have control: Why should we give it up?

We hunger for control.

We may trust food more than we trust people.

We hunger for companionship.

What do you hunger for?

Honoring the Hungering Self.

Love yourself.

Love yourself completely. Allow yourself to hear and understand your deepest desires. This may be where you are suffering.

Determine what you are hungering for. Make a list of ten or fifteen things you have always wanted to do. Is there one you can do? Right now?

Don't judge yourself.

Accept the freedom of the next step. Act.

Take the next step.

Sometimes the issue before us isn't how to begin to take a next step, but how to keep taking the next step.

The flow we were a part of when we made our promise is sometimes not there when we face the actual step. So, the problem is how to sustain the energy for change when we no longer feel that kind of energy. Suddenly, the old and the comfortable feel more attractive then the new and the challenging.

Become aware of how you control your body. Do you edit energy flow around any specific constellation of thoughts and feelings?

The actual next step is to find out what shapes your life more: Your will or your willfulness.

Your will is your desire to follow your goal/your energy. Your willfulness is your desire to resist your goal, your refusal to be told what to do, even by yourself. If it is your willfulness that shapes your life, you will not take the next step simply because you don't want to be forced to capitulate to your own dictates. You feel at some level you aren't ready to change.

Plan on getting up fifteen minutes earlier tomorrow for a spiritual practice.

*When we become vegetarians, we come to understand
that there is only now to be vegetarians.*

The time to do it is now, not tomorrow. There is only
now to be vegetarians, because one cannot be a vegetarian in
theory only. We are always doing it now because it is
integrated into our lives; we have developed the habit of
vegetarianism.

**Did you get up fifteen minutes earlier today? Did
you keep your promise?**

The Nowness of Vegetarianism.

Recognizing the "nowness of vegetarianism" is often easier for vegetarians because we have had practice at it. At some earlier time, at an earlier "now," we integrated the desire and the action for ourselves and became vegetarians. Nonvegetarians have not acted according to the understanding that there is only now to be vegetarians. Especially if they postpone indefinitely, they allow the energy of guilt, anxiety, and defensiveness to circulate. Nonvegetarians who postpone becoming vegetarians without creating some sort of practice toward that becoming—some setting in motion of the necessary foundation for becoming vegetarian (in other words paving the way for vegetarianism)— will never encounter the "now" in which vegetarianism occurs. What we know is that as we make the change to become and be vegetarians, it welcomes us.

Give a meat eater you know a gift certificate to a vegetarian restaurant.

I am connected to all that is.

My partner Bruce makes stained-glass windows. One window he created, "Our Town," faces the rising sun. In one corner of the window, the glass sun rises in a glorious splendor of reds, oranges, and yellows. In the opposite corner, the Earth, shaped in the Chinese symbol of yin and yang hovers in space. In the middle, a large star made of chandelier crystal ornaments is positioned. Around the star are old glass negatives. One shows two young children, another two dogs, another a woman. In the top corner above the Earth shines the moon, made of stones that were once weights in floral arrangements. In the morning, when the rising sun shines through the stained glass rising sun, a stream of colored light dances toward me. Later in the morning, the sun hits the crystal star and it sparkles. The moonstones create a soft glow; the negatives cause a light reversal. Through my spiritual practices, my own qualities have been burnished. Sometimes, like Bruce's sun, I radiate energy; sometimes like his star I refract it. Sometimes I am able to reverse things. Through my spiritual practice, I have experienced that the universe is "my town."

Go to a cathedral, church, synagogue, or other place of worship and appreciate the beauty of the light.

The very rhythms of cooking are meditative.

We stir and stir, changing the activity of the brain through repetitious motions. We meet our unconscious as we mix and chop. When your mind is tired, cooking may refresh it. The ritual of food preparation draws you in so that you let go of the external world. With the food itself—its taste, aroma, and appearance—and the sounds and actions of cooking or kneading or peeling, you stir yourself into the process.

If you like pasta, stock a variety of kinds: orzo, lasagna, zita. Have fun mixing vegetables, sauces, and pasta together.

A spiritual person cultivates the ability to be nonviolent
in every aspect of his or her life.

Touching the world, healing it, and repairing it in our daily actions is a spiritual practice. It is also a form of courage. Here is one more definition of vegetarianism: Believing in the small, invisible, daily path of peace.

Brainstorm what a gentle eating practice would be for you. Try it out.

Creating vegetarian food is the still point of the day.

As we commit ourselves to a practice of vegetarianism we discover that peace is a feeling that goes much deeper than we had realized. The doing of the work itself, the learning of the techniques of food preparation, the experience of creating vegetarian dishes offers us an opportunity to feel a sense of pleasure, peace, and harmony. In the midst of the apparent busy-ness of standing, stirring, mixing, stillness exists.

Select a favorite recipe that can be make vegan. Take the time to cook it. Notice how you are feeling as you cook.

By working with our dreams, we treat them as living aspects of our personality.

We honor the part of us that expresses itself through dreams. Dreams offer us wholeness. In the face of the healing nature of dreams, why should we settle for only fractions of a life?

Review your dreams: Have they changed over the past few months?

Cooking itself is not one act, but multiple acts in one:
Creation, affirmation, and sharing.

We cook with awareness because we are nourishing both body and soul. Preparing vegetarian food and eating it is a reminder that we need both physical and spiritual nourishment.

As you prepare a meal, explore how you are being nourished by providing nourishment.

We are linked with the rest of nature.

The inner art of vegetarianism is a spiritual practice that links us to the rest of nature and the rest of our own nature.

Close your eyes, breathe deeply, and allow the breath to help you release tension. When you feel relaxed, visualize yourself in an intricate web of relationships with other humans, animals, plants and the Earth. Give thanks for this connectedness.

Something positive exists and we can access it for ourselves.

We are the something positive that exists and we can unfold it, be its reflection and manifestation. In this way, we experience that the positive is not the outcome but the process.

Celebrate life! Your life and the life of all around you! Do it in your own way.

A spiritual person is powerful.

The habit of practice brings a part of the denied self into the present. We etch out time, or taste, to bring to consciousness this desire for wholeness and act upon it. In this process of integration, we discover that we are indeed powerful, empowered by being present to ourselves.

Be thankful to yourself for your inner art.

Sometimes our spiritual practice becomes the raft through the flood of crisis and trauma.

This is the gift of a spiritual practice. By learning how to cross the water, to raft from "then" to "now," we develop the ability to raft in even more turbulent waters. Tragedy is unplanned, unexpected, undesired change. But still it is change. And spiritual practice aligns itself with change. By conscientiously working with planned, expected, desired change—that is, establishing a next step and moving toward it—we are given the gift of surviving and growing when we are plunged into unplanned change.

Reach out to someone who is suffering today.

A spiritual person sustains a vision of defining what he or she is for while living deeply in touch with her or his own and the world's troubles.

Christina Baldwin, a wise writer and journal-keeper, observes, "To work in the world lovingly means that we are defining what we will be for, rather than reacting to what we are against." Together, compassion and nonviolence enable us to do the work of defining and the work of loving.

Ask yourself: How can I unfold my vision of what I am for in the next few days? Identify two simple acts that you can do and do them. Let love flow through you.

*Wholeness is when what we do for and with our body
and what do we for our soul are the same thing.*

I believe the body desires wholeness; if we can get our conditioned mind out of the way, we can unfold it. For instance, we breathe for both body and soul. Our breath unites them. We move in yoga for both body and soul, *asana* uniting them. We eat vegetarian; our body enacts the soul's truth: We are all connected.

Reflect on the meaning of wholeness in your journal or in a letter to yourself.

Doing the least harm, I discover joy for the Earth, for myself, for the animals.

Joy happens when we accept the gift of vegetarian consciousness and realize, not only, "I can live this way," but in living this way, I encounter a happiness that is deeper, freer, more expansive.

Today, I will see in my plant-based meal the abundance of love that is unfolding through my life.

"Now I can look at you in peace."

Together, vegetarianism and spiritual practice say, "I will not be violent to myself or others." Like many travelers, I did not become a vegetarian overnight, or by myself. I followed signs. I was embraced by loving vegetarians who helped me. I learned from vegetarian cookbook writers who chronicled their spiritual journey in and through their recipes. Animals helped me too. The Czech writer Franz Kafka said it best, "Now I can look at you in peace," he said to fishes. "I don't eat you anymore."

Close you eyes and imagine each species of animal that you have eaten in the past. As you bring the image of a cow, a pig, a fish, a rabbit, a deer, or whomever to your mind's eye, repeat, "Now I can look at you in peace, I don't eat you anymore."

> *The inner art of vegetarianism is a living* ahimsā, *the absence of violence.*

For many spiritual vegetarians, the word *ahimsā* guides our understanding of nonviolence. Christopher Key Chapple, a noted scholar of Asian religions, explains that *ahimsā* is not so much "nonviolence" as the "absence of the desire to kill or harm." The concept of *ahimsā* influences the practice of vegetarianism in the religions of Jainism, Buddhism, and Hinduism and in the yoga tradition. Chapple explains that nonviolent action presumes nondifference. I cultivate nonviolence within myself because I see myself connected to others.

By practicing a nonviolent diet, you automatically boycott many companies. Your resistance saves one chicken at lunch and one fish at dinner. See the animals being restored, one by one, by your enaction of *ahimsā*.

Peace in the Kitchen.

Once, in snowy western Minnesota, I came across a booth at a conference on nonviolence. The booth featured a quotation form Barbara Choo, "World peace starts right here. I will not raise my child to kill your child." I see that promise as including all the animals' children too.

Order a vegan take out meal and enjoy it in a festive room in your house.

Walk lightly upon the Earth.

We are Earthlings. Remember, the words "human" and "humus" come from the same root word. Our body is the Earth in a microcosm. Walk lightly upon the earth body that we inhabit.

Let rice grow.

A Meditation for the Winter Solstice.

Breathing in, I am aware of my animal body.

Breathing out, I release myself into the animal world.

Breathing in, I remember the natural.

Breathing out, I release myself into the natural world.

Breathing in, I am aware of the universe in my body.

Breathing out, I release myself into the universe.

In. Out.

Animal. Natural.

In. Out.

Remembering, releasing.

> **Sit still. If you feel your back slump, sit on a pillow or a chair. Repeat each couplet several times, feeling yourself becoming more centered. Continue through the meditation, devoting about fifteen minutes to it.**

Doing the least harm is a way to celebrate the miracle that is this Earth and this Self.

Doing the least harm, we can be open to and feel all the connections that emanate from within. We are coming together. Guilt and apology about our role in animals' deaths are released from clogging up the internal flow. Not being afraid of what we feel and what we experience, we can be completely present and completely aware. We can feel the sheer joy of walking this path, preparing life-giving food and being able to be open to the experience of cooking. We are integrating, constantly integrating. This is vital work.

Check in: Are outside demands keeping you from your vital work? Are you writing in your journal? Keeping your promises? Doing your vital work of making connections? How can you do the least harm to yourself and the Earth today?

Animals understand the individuality of other animals.

When my pony Jimmy died, his companion, Nicky, neighed, pawed, trotted around Jimmy's body, snorted, shook his head. After Jimmy was buried and I released Nicky into the pasture, he immediately galloped to the site where Jimmy died and neighed and snorted again. There is no reason for us not to believe that in every animal's life there is a Jimmy, a Nicky, a Babe the Pig, or a Rudolph the Red-Nosed Reindeer. With attention, we can experience this aspect of animals' lives— their individuality and their capacity for relationships.

Take a moment to think of animals who are mourning. Offer a prayer or a time of silence on their behalf.

*By paying attention to animals we acknowledge their
individuality.*

Rudolph the Red-Nosed Reindeer, like Bambi, like Babe
the Pig, or the chickens in "Chicken Run" have what
philosopher Tom Regan calls a biography. This is why the pigs
who played "Babe" in the movie were not eaten in real life.
They had a biography by association. They stop being
abstractions. The same process we bring to ourselves—refusing
to objectify ourselves, being attentive—we can bring to other
animals.

It is said that at midnight, on Christmas Eve, we can hear
the other animals talk. However, it is also said, anyone who
listens is driven mad. But there is another way of listening—it
is by coming to our senses. Each day we have the potential to
listen to the other animals with our hearts.

**Make a list of the animals you are thinking about
today.**

A Peace Meditation

Peace begins here, with my hands. I handle foods from the plant world.

Peace begins here with my eyes. I see the abundant plant world.

Peace begins with my heart. I will not take from you, animals, to feed me.

Peace begins with my spirit. I am awake to interconnections.

Peace begins here: I look, smell, touch, and am in tune with a rhythm of life.

Find a way, today, to keep peace in your heart, hands, and spirit.

On this grace I feed.

To be a vegetarian is to be a witness: I will do the least harm possible.

To be a vegetarian is to celebrate good food from the earth.

To be a vegetarian is to experience grace, and on this grace I feed.

What are the signs of grace in your life?

When your spiritual life is central to your living, that is when the earth shifts.

Do you have doubts, worries, or regrets? Don't let them discourage you; this is part of the journey. You may be feeling that the ground is shifting under you. That is because it is. You are changing the figure-ground relationship. What used to be the ground doesn't ground you anymore; what you are bringing into your life—what used to be the figure—does.

How have you changed this year? If you wrote yourself a letter on January 7, open it and read it now. Has your ground changed?

"The spirit won't drop you."

When the ground shifts underneath you, you may feel that you are facing an abyss. You do not feel grounded in practice. If you are facing your own abyss, let me pass on to you the life preserver I received from my friend Pat. At a time in my life when I felt ungrounded, she said to me, "Believe me, the spirit won't let you go. The spirit won't drop you." The spirit won't drop you because you are awake! Awakening creates its own energy.

Remind yourself that the spirit won't drop you as you take your next step.

There is no time like the present to change.

The Spirit won't drop you.
Just move forward—
    don't be scared
    don't be judgmental
    touch the process.

The spirit won't drop you because you are awake! The universe will meet you here.

Express gratitude for your life and your living and your place in the universe today.

I promise to keep practicing.

I promise to take time for myself. I promise to meet myself here—on the page, at the yoga mat, in the kitchen. There may be days when I don't practice. When the thread of awareness is dropped. But its absence will call me back. I will begin again. I will come home to myself. I promise I will keep practicing.

Today think of something you have completed and feel gratitude for your hard work, and think of someone who is beginning something.

Vegetarianism is both an object of change and a teacher
of how to change.

By deciding to become a vegetarian and then by
changing, you begin to experience the world in a more positive
way. You learn how to make a commitment through
vegetarianism, and then you learn how to keep a commitment.
Anyone who wants to change the world or themselves can
learn this too. Vegetarianism offers this to everyone.

And, if this year, this month, this day you did not change
as much as you wished—if your next step is clearly before
you—remember, tomorrow brings you a new day, a new
month, a new year, and with it the opportunity for a whole
new world.

Today, celebrate change by writing a letter to your
local newspaper inviting others to encounter the
life-changing nature of vegetarianism. Take this
book and prepare yourself to begin again the
following year, or adapt each of these reflections
to the concerns that have arisen for you
throughout the year.